THE SHAMAN'S PATH TO FREEDOM

Also by don Jose Ruiz

*Shamanic Power Animals: Embracing
the Teachings of Our Non-Human Friends*

*The Medicine Bag: Shamanic Rituals &
Ceremonies for Personal Transformation*

*The Wisdom of the Shamans: What the Ancient
Masters Can Teach Us about Love and Life*

THE SHAMAN'S PATH TO FREEDOM

<><><><><><><><><><><><><><><><><><><><><><><><><><><><><><><><><>
<><><><><><><><><><><><><><><><><><><><><><><><><><><><><><><><><>

A TOLTEC WISDOM BOOK

DON JOSE RUIZ

**Foreword by don Miguel Ruiz,
author of *The Four Agreements***

Hier⊕phantpublishing

Cover design by Adrian Morgan
Cover art by Shutterstock
Print book interior design by Frame25 Productions

Hierophant Publishing
San Antonio, TX
www.hierophantpublishing.com

If you are unable to order this book from your local bookseller,
you may order directly from the publisher.

Library of Congress Control Number: 2023940729
ISBN: 978-1-950253-39-5

10 9 8 7 6 5 4 3 2 1

CONTENTS

FOREWORD

When I tell people that my son Jose is an angel, I sometimes get some funny looks. But, as Jose writes in this
beautiful book, the English word *angel* comes from the
Greek word for "messenger." Ever since his initiation
into the Toltec lineage, Jose has transformed himself
into a messenger of unconditional love—and what
kind of angel could be more necessary at this moment
in human history?

Unconditional love is a force of liberation. It frees
us from the negative judgments we pass on ourselves
and others. It frees us from the illusion that we are separate from our fellow beings. Most important, it frees
us from the belief that we are "not enough." Once you
establish the habit of loving yourself and others unconditionally, many of the familiar problems of life drop
away. Instead of chasing a state of happiness that lies

always in the future, just out of reach, you realize that you have everything you need to be happy right here, right now. You wake up to the fact that this human life is a dream, and start to dream something beautiful.

For Jose, unconditional love has been key to his finding his own personal freedom. In the Toltec tradition, personal freedom means taking radical responsibility for your experience here on planet earth—in other words, realizing that you are the architect of your own dream. If you are used to believing that your words, actions, and emotions are "caused" by outside forces beyond your control, the concept of personal freedom may take a little getting used to. But once you start to practice it, using the wonderful exercises in this book, you will never want to go back to your old way of living.

The more you realize that you are the artist of your own life, the more resilient, more powerful, and more compassionate you become. In turn, this helps you develop your ability to love unconditionally. As Jose teaches in this book, personal freedom and unconditional love reinforce each other, creating a cycle of virtue. By cultivating unconditional love in our own hearts and minds, we can all overcome the mental habits of self-judgment, negativity, and fear, and transform ourselves into messengers of peace.

May the exercises in this book inspire and support you on your own path to freedom, and may your life be saturated with the wisdom of unconditional love. Nothing could be more important for humanity at this time.

Warmly,

don Miguel Ruiz

EXPLANATION OF KEY TERMS

Addiction to suffering: The mind's choice to suffer rather than to live in freedom. This is the current state of most human minds on the planet.

Domestication: The primary system of control in the Dream of the Planet. Starting when we are very young, we are presented with rewards or punishments that cause us to adopt the beliefs and behaviors that others find acceptable. Through this process, we are "domesticated," in the Toltec sense.

Dream of the Planet: The combination of every single being's Personal Dream. The Dream of the Planet constitutes the world we live in.

Nagual: A Nahuatl word with two meanings. It is used to identify Toltec shamans, and to describe the life force energy and divinity within all beings.

Nahuatl: Language of the ancient Toltec peoples.

Personal Dream: The unique reality created by every individual; your personal perspective. It is the manifestation of the relationship between your mind and your body.

Personal freedom: Toltecs achieve personal freedom when they take radical responsibility for their experiences and realize that they are the artists who create their own Personal Dreams.

Shamans: Those who are awakened to the realization that all beings are life force energy, and that humans are dreaming all the time.

Toltec/Artist: In the Toltec sense, every person is an artist and our lives are our art. The word *Toltec* means "artist" in Nahuatl.

Toltec warriors: Those who are committed to using the teachings of the Toltec tradition to win the inner battle against domestication and achieve their own personal freedom.

Unconditional love: A force of liberation that frees us from negative judgments, from the illusion that we are separate from our fellow beings, and from our own feelings of inadequacy.

THE TOLTEC PATH

Humanity is in crisis.

Almost everywhere we look, we see disharmony, injustice, cruelty, and destruction. When we let ourselves feel the pain of the wars and environmental catastrophes we see on TV or in our news feeds, it can seem almost too much to bear and we can soon feel overwhelmed and powerless. Sometimes it feels as if the best we can hope for is to seek security and comfort for ourselves and our loved ones, while closing our hearts to the overwhelming plight of others and of the planet.

But these problems are not new to the world. Across the generations, societies have wrestled with discord and violence, searching for ways to move beyond humanity's destructive instincts and realize its spiritual potential. One such civilization was that of the Toltecs.

The Toltecs flourished in what is now south-central Mexico between one and two thousand years ago. They built an advanced society whose people devoted significant time and energy to self-realization and spiritual practice. The later Aztec culture recognized them as their intellectual and cultural progenitors, and viewed Toltec civilization as superior to all others.

The Toltecs saw themselves as artists. Indeed, the word *Toltec* means "artist" in Nahuatl, the language of this ancient people. This culture produced some stunning achievements in painting, sculpture, and architecture, including the majestic Pyramids of the Sun and Moon just outside Mexico City. Yet the Toltec concept of artist is not confined to people who serve in these roles. To Toltecs, every person is an artist, and the goal of each of us is to live our lives in a way befitting the creation of a masterpiece.

The Toltecs developed a complex cosmology and lived a rich spiritual life. Like the Vedic people of India, they followed a path of self-realization, or what we call personal freedom. Although they did not leave behind written works of literature like the famous *Rig Veda*, their knowledge and beliefs have been passed down through oral tradition in the form of stories and practices that are still taught to this very day.

The Toltec path focused on the ability of each of us to bring about our own awakening, thereby contributing to the awakening of others. It taught that it was only by each individual finding his or her own personal freedom that humanity could achieve lasting change on a larger scale. In other words, to change the world, we must change ourselves.

Toltec Spirituality

Long ago, the shamans in my family realized that the human mind is dreaming all the time, because we can only ever see life through the filter of our own perceptions. In this way, life is a reflection of our own beliefs and conditioning. Toltec shamans call the unique reality created by each individual the Personal Dream, which is shaped by our personal perspectives and is the manifestation of the relationship between our minds and our bodies. These unique realities in turn combine to make the Dream of the Planet, which is made up of the Personal Dream of every single being in the world. This collective dream forms the basis for how we interact and communicate with one another, and is the foundation of what we perceive as the world in which we live. Unfortunately, as we look at the Dream of the Planet today, it appears in many ways to be a nightmare.

Yet, although there is great suffering all around us, there is also great beauty. Each of us is born with a divine light within. Spiritual traditions from around the world have given this light many names—the soul, *jiva*, the source, the life force. In the Toltec tradition, we call this light the *nagual*, and we believe that we all possess this divine force in equal amounts.

Like many words in other languages, however, the Nahuatl word *nagual* has a second meaning. It also means "the awakened one," or "shaman." While Toltecs believe that we all possess the light of nagual by virtue of our innate divinity, they define a shaman as a person who has become aware of this divinity, who cultivates this inner light with skill and intention, and in doing so achieves their own *personal freedom*. They can then focus their energy on creating a Dream of the Planet that is beautiful rather than a nightmare, becoming peacemakers, community builders, and servants of all living beings. This is why Toltecs place such a high value on personal freedom, and bestow the title of *nagual* upon those who achieve it.

Personal Freedom

Most people today live in a state of fear and anxiety. They may not be aware that they are fearful and anxious, but those feelings are there, lurking just beneath the surface. They are afraid of being judged, of being shamed, of losing their identities, of failing to measure up to some imaginary standard. Rather than being free, most are enslaved to the pursuit of some temporary feeling of security, acceptance, or material comfort.

But the path of a nagual is different. It is characterized by two key elements: personal freedom and unconditional love. In fact, these two qualities are largely one and the same. When you show unconditional love toward yourself and others, you automatically become free, because your life is no longer defined by judgment, fear, and negativity. Conversely, when you do the hard work of freeing your mind from judgment, fear, and negativity, you naturally uncover a wellspring of unconditional love.

When you have personal freedom, you're comfortable in your own skin. You don't fear others' judgment, because you have long since given up the practice of judging yourself. You don't fear specific outcomes—changing jobs, losing a partner, moving to a new location—because you know that wherever you go, whatever you do, and whomever you're with, you're still life force energy itself. Pure, unadulterated nagual energy. No matter what happens, you never stop being anything less than *life*.

Another characteristic of personal freedom is the ability to look into the eyes of others and see yourself—really see yourself, with no separation. Although it's easy to say that we are all connected, it's another thing to feel it on a visceral level. Every time you take a breath, you breathe in the same air that sustains the lives of all your brothers and sisters here on earth. When you enjoy the feeling of the sun on your skin, you feel the same warmth that every human and animal on the planet feels. You share in the same energy that the sun gives to every plant and tree. The water you drink has quenched the thirst of many others before you. When you remember these truths, you break down the illusion of separation.

The ability to see—and, more important, *to feel*—this connection to nature is perhaps one of the qualities for which shamans are best known. Not only do shamans appreciate the sighing of the trees and the crashing of the ocean waves, but we know that we, too, *are nature*. The same beauty that we perceive in plants and animals exists in us as well. Once you realize this, you are free from the illusions of ugliness and unworthiness. A flower cannot be ugly. An ocean cannot be unworthy. Neither can you.

In the Toltec tradition, we say that *everyone* has the capacity to access this state of personal freedom and become a shaman. Most of us, however, have to face one giant obstacle on this path to freedom—the mind's addiction to suffering, which causes us to choose to suffer rather than to live in freedom.

Huitzilopochtli and Quetzalcoatl

In pre-Columbian Mesoamerica, one of the most popular gods was Huitzilopochtli, the god of war.

Although his followers came from different places and called him by different names, they all had one thing in common. They inflicted suffering on others through violence and war. And they practiced human sacrifice to appease him. In Toltec cosmology, Huitzilopochtli is the brother of the better-known god Quetzalcoatl, whose symbol is a feathered serpent. Unlike his brother, Quetzalcoatl is a redeeming, loving figure who inspires many of the practices we still use today.

In one story, Quetzalcoatl lures his brother into a cave containing a magic waterfall in which Huitzilopochtli sees a reflection of the fanatical actions of his followers and the suffering they are causing in his name. In a moment of clarity, he drops to his knees and begs his brother for forgiveness. Quetzalcoatl forgives him, but tells him he must go and tell his followers that violence is not the way. Huitzilopochtli does as he's told but soon discovers that his followers are unwilling to give up war and human sacrifice because they have become addicted to it.

According to the shamans in my family, this addiction to suffering continues to afflict humanity to this day. Just like any other addiction, it can cause us to seek out that which is harmful to us, in exchange for a temporary experience of satisfaction, security, or relief. For example, we may judge others in order to feel better about ourselves temporarily, not realizing that these negative judgments poison our own minds as well. The deeper we fall into our addiction to suffering, the more we sacrifice our personal freedom and our capacity for unconditional love, until we can hardly remember what it felt like to live in any other way.

There is little doubt that the actions of Huitzilopochtli's fanatical followers contributed heavily to the downfall of their culture, leaving many of the once proud cities of the region in ruins. This is why Toltec shamans work to enlist Toltec warriors—those who do inner battle to end the illusion of separation, break the mind's addiction to suffering, and achieve personal freedom.

When I think of the story of Huitzilopochtli, I can't help but see the similarities between the civilizations of Mesoamerica and our own. We too are living in an era of self-inflicted suffering, but it doesn't have to be this way. We can all make the choice to become Toltec warriors. We can all do our part by rejecting the forces of greed, selfishness, and violence, and choosing the path of unconditional love. Let's hope we can do so before our civilization is destroyed as well.

How to Use This Book

This book is a radical invitation to break your mind's addiction to suffering, embrace unconditional love, and claim the personal freedom that is your birthright. To help you do that, I've identified ten key elements of personal freedom:

- ◆ The freedom to love yourself and others unconditionally.

- ◆ The freedom to heal from old wounds, no matter how long they've been with you.

- ◆ The freedom to change and allow those around you to change.

- ◆ The freedom to feel a full range of emotions and receive the gifts they offer.

- ◆ The freedom to see past your blind spots and gain a broader perspective.

- The freedom to dream with the awareness that you are dreaming.

- The freedom to care for your physical body.

- The freedom to accept life as it is.

- The freedom to forgive yourself and those who have hurt you.

- The freedom to serve those around you.

Although I have organized these freedoms in a way that I feel will be helpful to most readers, especially those who are new to the Toltec path, each chapter stands on its own. You don't have to read the book in order. If you feel that one particular strand of personal freedom is calling to you right now, turn to that chapter and begin there.

While reading about personal freedom is helpful in that it increases our awareness, its greatest benefits come when we incorporate these freedoms into our daily lives. I have included exercises at the end of each chapter to help you put these freedoms into practice. Some of these exercises include writing, so

I encourage you to get a journal reserved just for this purpose. Because many of these exercises are rituals, it's important to mention that, in shamanism, rituals are designed to work at a level deeper than your dreaming mind. This means that you should do them even if your mind objects or tries to convince you they are silly or will never work. Remember in these moments to be skeptical of your mind, which can be very sneaky in its efforts to maintain the status quo—including its addiction to suffering.

Throughout this book, you will find anecdotes and pearls of wisdom from Buddhism, Hinduism, and other spiritual traditions. Sometimes, people ask me why I include these stories in my books, since they are "not Toltec." We live in a very special time, when cultures around the world are sharing their sacred knowledge with one another. Although I was raised in the Toltec lineage, I've been blessed to travel all over the world, receiving spiritual wisdom from many other traditions and incorporating this wisdom into my own spiritual practice. All religious traditions are the many faces of the divine, and we are lucky to live in an age when we have access to so many of these beautiful faces. I have found that there is no need to put up walls between ideas and practices that are "Toltec" and "not Toltec," because all spiritual practice springs from the same eternal source, and all can teach us something about personal freedom and unconditional love.

In the Toltec tradition, we know that each of us has our own innate divinity, but sometimes the light within us is obscured and we need a guide to help us find our way back home. My hope is that this book can serve as a guide to finding the truth that is already within you. It doesn't matter how long you've been wandering around in the fog, cut off from the sacredness of your life. The light of the nagual is still within you, and you can reconnect with it starting right now, today. When you do this, you end or greatly lessen your own suffering and elevate all of humanity at the same time. This is the most important thing you can do for the Dream of the Planet at this time.

Chapter 1

THE FREEDOM TO LOVE

Imagine you have been tasked with caring for a six-month-old baby. If you are like most people, you will automatically treat this baby with unconditional love and kindness. Even if the baby screams and throws its spoon on the floor, you will keep on speaking to it gently, taking care of it, and giving it only love and kindness. No matter what the child does, you won't take it personally, because you know this is just what babies do.

It is easy to feel unconditional love for a baby, because it is so obvious that the child is innocent, vulnerable, and completely unaware of the consequences of its actions. By feeding this baby a steady stream of love, you teach it that the world is a safe place and give it the best possible opportunity to grow and develop.

The shamans in my family's Toltec tradition have taught for millennia that unconditional love is the greatest power a human being possesses, and that is why we will begin our journey together with an examination of its unique power. When you live in unconditional love, insults, judgments, and angry rhetoric can't touch your heart, because you can see that even the most vicious of these attacks are no more personal than a six-month-old baby throwing a spoon on the floor. Unconditional love is the key to personal freedom.

As children, many of us were lucky enough to receive unconditional love from our parents or from some other significant figure in our lives. Yet even the most well-meaning parents or caregivers eventually slip into using love in a conditional way, as a tool for reward and punishment. In the Toltec tradition, we refer to this as "domestication."

Domestication is the process by which we assimilate into the society in which we live. For example, we learn to say "please" and "thank you," to take off our shoes before entering the house, and to bring a gift when we visit someone's home. This kind of domestication isn't inherently positive or negative—in fact, it's a normal and necessary process. If we weren't domesticated in some basic ways, it would be hard to communicate with the people around us or participate in society. However, in some cases, domestication can be used in a way that is negative, and when this happens, it can cause us to forget our connection to the nagual within.

For instance, as we grow up, many of us learn that if we behave in a certain way, we will receive a reward—love—and if we don't behave in a certain way, we will receive a punishment—the withholding of love. In some instances, we may receive something even worse than the mere withholding of love—shame. Unfortunately, shame is an extremely effective tool for domesticating others.

There are likely people in your life who withheld their love or even shamed you during your formative years for talking, dressing, or acting in a certain way. As a result, you learned that, if you wanted to receive their love, you had better avoid those behaviors. This is not to say that you should feel anger or hostility toward your parents or caregivers, who often carried out this domestication in an effort to protect you from societal judgments or with the intention to be helpful. In all cases, they were simply repeating what was done to them, as the process of domestication has been going on from generation to generation for thousands of years.

Over time, we become so conditioned by the process of domestication that our original domesticators no longer need to be present. We start to withhold love from ourselves or even shame ourselves when we don't live up to the ideals instilled in us by others. This is what the shamans in my family refer to as "self-domestication."

Once we begin to self-domesticate, the process of domestication is complete. We berate ourselves internally for a litany of reasons, but the common denominator is the "not enough" monster, which represents the ways in which we don't measure up to our domesticated ideals. If we are not as successful, as attractive, or as functional as we feel we "should" be, we try to motivate ourselves to do better through self-shaming and other forms of negative self-talk. But shaming and arguing with yourself are just as effective as arguing with a six-month-old baby—the baby responds to love, not to logic, and this is truer of adults than you may suppose.

Thanks to our domestication, we are like the elephant whose foot is chained to a pole when it is first born. As a baby, the elephant is not strong enough to break the chain, no matter how hard it tries. As an adult, the elephant has the power to break the chain at any time but doesn't even try, because it believes it is impossible. It has self-domesticated to a state of powerlessness. Indeed, it might not walk away even if the chain were removed!

This is the trap of domestication and conditional love. But there is a way out. By committing to seeing the nagual that resides in yourself and everyone else, you can begin to love yourself and others unconditionally. This is the key to overcoming any negative domestications you have internalized.

The Challenges of Love

Loving others unconditionally does not mean that you never disagree with them or feel frustrated by their actions. It also doesn't mean pandering to them, letting them violate your boundaries, or saying "yes" to their requests when in your heart the answer is "no." What unconditional love *does* mean is continuously extending your benevolence toward others and toward yourself, even in the midst of conflict or disagreement. It means refusing to contract into fear, hatred, or suffering, or to take action from a place of negativity, even when you are being strongly provoked. And it means making consistent attempts to bring your highest self to every interaction, while continuously seeking to connect with what's highest and best in others. While it can be incredibly difficult to do so in some situations, you can become a master at it through practice.

For example, a schoolteacher may feel frustrated by a student's repeated attempts to disrupt the class. If she is coming from a place of conditional love, she may label the student as "bad" and treat him or her as being less worthy than other students. If she is coming from a place of unconditional love, she will continue to treat the student with respect and attempt to reach the nagual within, even as she addresses the disruptive behavior. Unconditional love is like the ocean floor. No matter what the waves are doing on the surface, the ocean floor is always there, and no amount of stormy weather is going to wash it away.

Unconditional love is often hardest to achieve when it comes to yourself. Many of us feel intense frustration toward ourselves in certain moments—for example, right after we've locked the keys in the car, or made an awkward comment, or failed to live up to a promise or goal. Although your first mental reaction may be to self-scold, unconditional love means continuously extending benevolence toward yourself, even when you've done something you regret or that your mind steps in and tells you is "bad" or "foolish."

The Hunt for Love

The shamans in my family taught that we are all like hunters, searching for love outside ourselves. We hunt for love in other humans, not realizing that they are also hunting for love in us. They don't love themselves either—at least not unconditionally—so they're hoping that we can fill that need for them, just as we're hoping they can fill it for us. In this sense, we're all like drug addicts going around to see if anybody has any drugs for us, while the people we're asking are simultaneously hoping that *we* have drugs for *them*!

The truth is that when you find love, it always comes from within yourself, *not* from others. If you don't believe me, just think of all the moments in your life when someone loved you, and yet you persisted in feeling unloved. As a child or teenager you may have felt unloved when your parents did not allow you to go somewhere with your friends or stay out after a certain time at night. But this feeling of being unloved was a subjective state, not an accurate reflection of your parents' love or lack of love. As an adult, you may have felt unloved if your partner did not make the romantic gesture you longed for. Yet all the while, your partner's love for you may have been very intense indeed. In other words, our feelings of being loved or unloved come from inside us, not from the outside world.

A friend of mine had a brother with many deep emotional wounds that made it difficult for him to feel and receive love. Although she showered him with love when they were together—cooking for him, helping him around the house, and engaging him in long conversations about his life—he always questioned whether or not she "really" loved him. To an outside observer, it was clear that the problem lay in his inability to receive love, not in his sister's inability to give it. He was like a cell phone that couldn't pick up a signal, even though the signal was extremely strong.

It was only when he adopted a dog that his ability to give and receive love began to develop. The dog was always happy to see him, no matter what. He realized that the dog loved him unconditionally, and he loved the dog back. The ability to receive love from an animal created warmth in his heart and paved the way for him to love himself and receive love from other sources as well. Although it took him a long time, he was eventually able to smile at his sister and say, "Thank you so much for calling to wish me happy birthday. I know you love me and I appreciate you taking the time to express it."

It is your *own* love that makes you able to perceive and receive the love of others. The more you cultivate your own capacity to love unconditionally, the more you develop the ability to pick up a strong "love signal" wherever you go. At the same time, no matter how much you develop your own capacity for love, you can never force another person to feel or receive your love. It's impossible to "make" another person happy, because happiness always comes from within. You can do kind things for others, but you cannot control their ability to receive those kindnesses. This is why making yourself responsible for another person's happiness is a surefire way to generate suffering.

You Are the Love of Your Life

The one person for whose happiness you *can* be responsible is—you guessed it!—*you*. By developing your capacity to perceive, receive, and generate love, you can make yourself happy, and therefore have more to offer the people around you. Although it may sound odd or unconventional, *you* are the love of your life— not your boyfriend or girlfriend, your husband or wife. You are the one person to whom you have complete and total access, twenty-four hours a day. Your physical body is the one body on the planet for which you are completely responsible; your heart the only heart, your mind the only mind. You can take care of yourself in a way that nobody else can—and this is true of every other human being as well.

Seeing yourself as the love of your life is much easier said than done, however, as most of us have a deep-seated aversion to this idea. Many of us have been domesticated to be much harder on ourselves than we are on anyone else. We learn that it is "good" to scold and disparage ourselves. But this only reinforces the powerful idea that we are not good enough, or not attractive enough, or not smart enough to be worthy of the kind of intense, unconditional love we readily offer to a baby or an animal, or even an adult we cherish. In shamanic terms, we can say that almost all of humanity is under a negative hex or spell.

How can we break this spell? It takes practice and commitment, and it starts with treating yourself the same way you would treat a beloved partner, a child, a family member, or a favorite furry friend. Think of someone for whom you feel intense, unconditional love. Can you imagine feeling the exact same way about *yourself*? For many of us, this is very difficult—it may even feel deeply taboo. Maybe you fear that loving yourself will make you arrogant, self-indulgent, or worse. The first time you truly allow yourself to experience self-love can be an incredibly emotional experience—you may cry or feel very vulnerable.

To begin to forge a relationship with the love of your life, ask yourself: What does this being want? What do they like? What are their passions? What do they need to thrive? How can I help them experience all these things?

The love of my life is named Jose. I keep Jose happy by playing the guitar and creating art; he loves doing that. Jose loves music, especially rock and roll. Going to a rock concert is a meditation for him. He also feels happy when he carries out his calling in life, which is to help others by teaching and passing on the wisdom from his family's traditions. He loves sharing his heart and his life experiences with others. And when he can share his heart *and* his music, that's when he feels the perfect equilibrium and the most happiness in life.

Maybe it sounds silly to talk about yourself in the third person, but doing so can help you break the spell of domestication. That's because most of us would never judge another person the way we judge ourselves. Speaking about yourself in the third person helps break the habit of self-flagellation, which is just another expression of the mind's addiction to suffering. I have included an exercise at the end of this chapter to help you develop this skill.

Every day, I remind myself that I am pure life—nagual energy—perfect and complete in this moment. I have also been given this specific body and this particular personality and this particular name. I've been given this expression of the nagual that is Jose to care for, and taking care of Jose is my number one task in this lifetime. Taking care of this creature is a sacred responsibility. Once you realize this, your whole life begins to change.

To Thine Own Self Be True

Have you ever watched children playing, and noticed how much of their play consists of assigning roles to themselves and others? "You be the cop, and I'll be the robber." And they get very upset when somebody breaks the rules of these agreements. "You're supposed to be the robber, and the robber wouldn't do this or that. Do it *my* way!"

Adults can express this same indignation when we decline to play the roles they have in mind for us. "You're supposed to be the spiritual guy!" "You're supposed to be the one with the happy marriage!" The shamans of my family teach that there is no point in getting angry at people for trying to hook us into their dreams. After all, they don't even realize they're dreaming! But if you have the awareness to know you are dreaming, you can feel compassion for them. You can say "no" without attacking them. You can acknowledge their requests and demands, and then continue to do what is necessary for your own life.

When I began my shamanic work in earnest, some told me that I had to stop listening to rock and roll, stop watching movies, and commit to the "spiritual path." So for a while, I did exactly that. I stopped listening to the music I loved. I stopped going to rock concerts. And I spent hours every day in a dark room, meditating with my eyes closed. I thought this was the "spiritual way." Before long, however, I was very unhappy, because I was neglecting the love of my life. I was going against myself by following someone else's dream of what it meant to be spiritual. But it wasn't *my* dream.

When I realized this, I began letting go of this "spiritual" persona. I discovered that I could satisfy my own heart—listen to my music, go to my rock concerts, and come out of the dark room and meditate with my eyes open. This is the spiritual path for Jose. With this realization, I started to take care of Jose again—the Jose who loves puppies, Guns N' Roses, and Vedic philosophy. The Jose who loves to travel and enjoys vegan food.

My father once told me that, while some spiritual seekers are obsessed with being serious, it is our child-like energy that helps us enjoy life. I love my rock and roll lifestyle. I am living my dream and I'm happy doing what I love. But this only became possible after I realized that taking care of Jose was the most important task in my life. It's not secondary. It's not self-indulgent. In fact, it's only by being true to Jose that I am most able to help others.

We can all learn to decline the roles others assign to us in their dreams. And we can learn to respond gracefully when others decline some aspect of our own dreams. Instead of blaming or attacking others for making us characters in their stories, we can listen calmly, remembering that all people are dreaming all the time. We can be Toltec warriors—those who have achieved mastery over themselves, and therefore have no need to dominate others.

When someone else tries to impose their dream on you and it creates a strong emotion inside, you can decline skillfully and at an appropriate time, instead of lashing out in a careless or haphazard way. You can say: "I hear that you wanted me to stay in this relationship, but I've made the decision to leave." When you speak in this way, you express your truth, while refraining from using emotional poison to hurt others, or shaming them for the contents of their own personal dreams.

The Barriers to Love

Even though we are made of the nagual, or pure life and infinite potential, we often see something limited and specific when we look at ourselves in the mirror. This is one of the challenges of inhabiting a body in the phenomenal world. In my own case, when I looked at myself in the mirror many years ago, I saw a person who had misused drugs and alcohol and been a victim of sexual abuse. I saw a cardboard character dogged by mistakes and failures—a hopeless loser who couldn't change. There were times when I couldn't even stand the sight of myself, and I wanted to break the mirror! I was a living example of the spiritual law that states that the greatest barriers to love are the ones we place in our own way.

I used these negative reflections to hurt myself and withhold love from myself. But by treating myself in this way, I was also spreading emotional poison to the people in my life. As my brother, don Miguel Ruiz Jr., likes to say: "We cannot give what we do not have." If I don't love myself unconditionally, I can't offer unconditional love to others. And the opposite is true as well. When I domesticate myself, I can't help but domesticate others, and this always results in some form of emotional poison. In this way, we inadvertently add to the negative energy in the Dream of the Planet.

I don't say this to make you feel guilty for the times you've spread negative energy without realizing it. We all do this from time to time. I share this to make the point that the best way we can help others and the planet is to love ourselves, befriend ourselves, and stop self-domesticating.

Another barrier to love is that many of us think that we can't love ourselves until we have accomplished some goal or reached a particular level of spiritual attainment. We think that we can't love ourselves until somebody else loves us or forgives us. But this is simply more domestication in disguise. The best time to start loving yourself is *right now*, in this very moment, regardless of what you've done or the mistakes you've made. If you find yourself in a leaky boat, the time to start bailing is always *right now*. Don't wait until you find the perfect bailer, or until you've figured out where the boat is heading. Just bail the water and patch the leak, because it's only when you've fixed your own boat that you can start saving others who are drowning.

I have learned that I don't need to justify my love or explain it. I just need to practice love. When you try to justify or explain your love, you create a tower of reasoning that others can tear down—or worse, that you can tear down using your own self-doubt. "Why do I love that person if they don't love me back?" "How can I forgive that person after what she did to me?" But when you stop trying to justify love and just practice it, nothing can stand in your way.

Exercise: Loving Kindness, Toltec Style

A practice I return to again and again is sending love out into the world. Many spiritual traditions have some form of this practice. Buddhists practice *metta*, or loving kindness meditation, in which they visualize a loved one, a stranger, or even a person who has hurt them, and wish them health, happiness, and peace. Catholics pray for the poor, the sick, and those in need. Yogis send love into the world by chanting mantras, playing instruments, or even by dancing.

The common thread among all these traditions is that you do not have to be physically present with a person or group to send love to them. You don't even have to know them! You just have to generate the energy of benevolence and love within your own heart, and the intention that this love will benefit others. All of these practices begin with sending love to yourself—wishing yourself health, happiness, and freedom from suffering—so that you can extend that love to others.

Here is my favorite way of sending love into the world, Toltec style:

- ◆ Rub your hands together until you feel some heat and energy building up between them.

- ◆ Visualize all the people in the world who are in need of love at this moment—the sick, the lonely, the vulnerable, and all those who are suffering.

- ◆ Reach out your hands and imagine the warmth and energy you just generated flowing out to these people, wherever they are and whatever their situation may be.

- Imagine this warmth and energy soothing their pain, easing their suffering, and giving them all the love they need.

- Bring your hands to your heart and let some of this warmth flow into your own body, filling you with the energy of love.

Doing this practice every day can help you develop your ability to love unconditionally, spreading happiness to yourself and everyone around you.

Exercise: Constant Kindness

Being truly kind means learning to nurture the seeds of goodness in yourself and in others. It represents a commitment to seeing others in a positive light, even when they are doing something you don't like. And just as we can send love to people we have never met, we can extend kindness to ourselves and those around us at every moment of every day.

Although we can practice kindness with everyone we meet, it is especially important to practice it with ourselves. If you want to get to a place of unconditional love, a practice of constant kindness will start you on the path.

- For the next twenty-four hours, consider all the ways in which you can appreciate yourself—your body, your appearance, your intellectual and artistic gifts, and the benefits you provide to your loved ones and your community.

- Every time you think of it, acknowledge your own goodness verbally or in writing.

- Whether or not you make these statements out loud, be sure to make them as frequently as possible throughout the day.

- Notice all the ways in which you are wonderful, helpful, beautiful, talented, hardworking, and sincere.

- Send a current of warmth toward yourself at all times.

For a friend of mine, this practice took the form of playful verbal exclamations. When she looked in a mirror, she exclaimed: "Damn, I'm cute!" When she tasted the soup she was cooking, she said: "Man, can I cook." Although there was an element of humorous grandiosity to these exclamations, they were, at the same time, sincere. As she continued with this practice, she realized that she was sending a steady current of kindness toward herself at all times, even when she wasn't expressing appreciation out loud. If you're like my friend, you just may find that you want to extend this practice beyond twenty-four hours and into the rest of your life.

When you are firmly established in the practice of extending constant kindness to yourself, it becomes easier to extend this loving energy toward everyone around you—to sincerely appreciate others, including those with whom you may not otherwise feel a connection, or even those you may dislike. From there, it is only the smallest of steps to move from kindness to unconditional love.

Chapter 2

THE FREEDOM TO HEAL

When I was a young teenager, I attended my father's Toltec apprenticeship classes, where students sat in a circle and passed around a large stick adorned with eagle feathers. When the stick came to you, it was your turn to speak.

I noticed that, many times, when adult apprentices got the stick, they chose to share a story of great suffering, prompting a chorus of "Ohhs" and "Ahhhhs" from the others. It seemed to me as if they were competing to determine who had suffered the most! When the stick came to me, I didn't know what to say, because I didn't have any sad stories to tell. I felt embarrassed by my lack of tragic tales, and thought I had better go out and find a way to suffer so that I, too, could become an adult.

Out of all the addictions to which we humans are vulnerable, the addiction to suffering is the most prevalent—especially in the West, where we are brought up on a steady diet of conflict and drama. Music, art, and movies glamorize incidents of heartbreak, violence, and tragedy, and we learn to highlight these experiences in our own lives. We treasure our stories of suffering, and cling to them tightly. When life is going well, we regularly go off in search of more suffering, just to keep things interesting. We give suffering a kind of prestige—the drug-addicted artist, the trauma survivor who writes a best-selling memoir—and feel anxious if our own suffering doesn't measure up to that of our idols.

When we're not aware of alternatives, this can feel like a totally normal way to live. Sixty years ago, it was considered normal to smoke cigarettes on airplanes and in crowded restaurants, behavior that would now be considered rude and that we now know is unhealthy. I think that someday we will look back at our culture's addiction to suffering and see it in the same way—as a very bizarre and unhealthy behavior that is best consigned to the past. Thanks to our addiction to suffering, we are all like airplane passengers in the 1960s, breathing in clouds of black smoke without even realizing there's a better way to live.

As long as you are addicted to anything, you cannot be free. Addiction keeps your energy tied up in the endless quest for more of the addictive substance or behavior, whether that's drugs, or love, or suffering. And as long as your energy is flowing into your addiction, it can't flow into the parts of your life that really need attention—opening your heart, shedding your old agreements, and creating a masterpiece that brings happiness to you and everyone around you. To progress on the path to freedom, you must become aware of your addiction to suffering and make the decision to heal.

Healing Old Wounds

When we're addicted to suffering, we keep splitting our old wounds open again and again, preventing them from healing. Often, this happens because we're afraid that, if we heal, we will lose our identities. This was certainly true for me. For many years, I needed to see myself as a victim—first of drug addiction, then of sexual abuse, and then of a bad marriage. It feels crazy to say this now, but I was truly frightened of giving up my old, familiar wounds. Who would I be without the stories that had defined me since the age of thirteen? It would be like walking out on the street naked—a scary and vulnerable feeling.

A friend of mine experienced this in a very real way. As a young teenager, she was captivated by stories of artists and poets who suffered from mental illness. She got hooked on the idea that, to be a great artist, you had to have a tragic and difficult life. By the time she was nineteen, she'd maneuvered herself into a diagnosis of mental illness and created her own dream of life as a tortured poet. This dream caused her a great deal of suffering, but she clung to it for years because she believed it was necessary in order to succeed as an artist.

By the time she was in her late twenties, however, that dream began to wear thin. She had known for a long time that she did not, in fact, have a mental illness. But she still clung to that identity because she saw it as a badge of honor, the same way my victim identities had been a badge of honor for me. When she finally made the decision to drop her old agreements about the necessity of suffering for her art, it was like smoke clearing. She realized that she was perfectly interesting just the way she was. She didn't need to go hunting for suffering she could use as a kind of trophy to show off to her friends. Just being a regular person was enough.

If you've created an identity out of your drama, your disappointments, and your problems, it can be difficult to take the first step in changing your dream. "What will people think if they see me smiling?" you may ask yourself. "They may think that my life has been easy. But it hasn't been easy, not at all." Maybe you're afraid that people won't respect you if they don't know how much you've suffered. You may fear that you'll seem immature and childlike, or that you'll lose something valuable if you give up your old wounds. However, this is not true.

The defining quality of true shamans—or of spiritual masters in other traditions—is their joy, not their suffering. Think of the spiritual masters you've met in your own life. Their eyes sparkle. They seem to radiate light with their whole being. They aren't slumped over, caught in a dream of their own woundedness. They move peacefully through the world, shining their light on everyone they see. Western culture tells us that happiness is fleeting and childish, while suffering is a sign of maturity and "the way things really are." But, in fact, the opposite is true. The real sign of maturity is joy, not suffering. The real mark of progress on the shaman's path is increasing lightness, not weight.

From Wounds to Wonder

In the Toltec tradition, we say there is nothing to learn, there is only "unlearning"—leaving behind suffering and the negative consequences it brings.

I'll never forget the trip I took to India when I was seventeen years old. One day, when I was on my way to the temple, I came across a holy man who was dancing and singing in the town square. A pair of Indian businessmen were standing nearby, watching him.

"Look at him!" said one. "I think he's crazy."

"He's in love with life," said the other.

"Are you in love with life?" the first asked.

"No," the second admitted.

"So, who's crazy?" the first replied.

Unlearning suffering lets us become like this holy man, in love with our lives. Like the holy man dancing and singing, we can stop spreading emotional poison and instead share joy and light with those around us.

We can become messengers of life instead of death, of love instead of despair. But we can only do this when we give up our addiction to suffering. And the first step to "unlearning" this addiction is to recognize the ways in which we are still holding on to our wounds.

In the Toltec tradition, we teach that humans often hold on to our wounds in the following ways:

Being careless with our word. When we are careless with our word, we tell lies to ourselves and to others. "I'm worthless." "I can't change." "I can never forgive myself or anybody else." We create the perfect environment in which our wounds can continue to fester indefinitely. Likewise, when we engage in gossip—"I wonder what my ex is up to." "Can you believe my dad did that?"—we rip open our wounds and prevent them from ever healing over.

Taking things personally. When we take things personally, wounds that might have stopped hurting long ago start to hurt again—like pouring alcohol on an open sore and making it sting even more. "How can she say that? She knows I'm sensitive about my looks." "How could he be so careless? I needed him to be there, and he didn't show up." When we do this, we take a tiny amount of pain and amplify it until we have all the pain we could ever want. This can keep wounds hurting for years after they would naturally have healed on their own.

Making assumptions. When we make assumptions, intentionally selecting the things most likely to hurt us, we close ourselves off to possibilities that might help us or heal us—like hunter-gatherers filling our baskets with only the most poisonous plants and fruits. "I'm sure she doesn't like me. I don't think he wants to hear from me after all these years." "They excluded me from their gathering because I'm not good enough." Assumptions like these form a protective barrier around our wounds, preventing any medicine from getting to them.

Refraining from doing our best. We tend to hold on to our wounds most tightly when we are on the verge of change. Because we're afraid to let go of the familiar, we don't do our best or even mess things up intentionally, hoping to buy ourselves more time in our comfort zone. We decide to be less courageous than we know we can be, or we stop just short of making an important change that could help us move forward in our lives. We protect our wounds by doing less than our best, because we know that our best will start to heal them.

Many of you will recognize the principles above from *The Four Agreements*, the best-selling book by my father, don Miguel Ruiz. What you may not know is that these agreements are really the story of his own awakening, as he overcame his own addiction to suffering by practicing those four agreements in every area of his life.

Later, when I recognized another way in which I was perpetuating my suffering, my father and I co-wrote a book called *The Fifth Agreement,* in which we presented another way in which we hold on to our wounds—by listening to and believing the mind's stories of negativity and failing to be skeptical of these delusions.

We all have delusions that support our wounds. Without them, our wounds would heal and vanish in no time. We project these delusions onto others, practically forcing them to hurt us in the ways we want or need to be hurt. For example, if you have a wound concerning betrayal, you may seek out people and situations in which you are all but guaranteed to be betrayed, and then say to yourself: "This always happens to me!" But when you do this, you fail to recognize that you ignored the warning signs that were there all along. If you have a wound concerning unworthiness, you may use other people to make yourself feel unworthy. For example, you may actively look for ways in which you feel slighted or ignored, and choose to interpret these actions in a hurtful light—even when other interpretations are possible.

In the Bible, Jesus tells his followers: "The truth will set you free." And, in fact, this idea is expressed beautifully in many different spiritual traditions. But another truth is that most people don't want to be free; they want to remain in habitual suffering. When you make the choice to heal from your old wounds, you break a spell that you placed on yourself weeks, months, or even years ago—believing that your wounds define you and are so central to your identity that you cannot live without them. Once that spell is broken, you stop spreading pain and suffering, and you begin to shine. You fall in love with life, and your life becomes a beautiful masterpiece of art.

Exercise: Noticing the Mind's Addiction to Suffering

Our minds tend to seek out what is familiar. Unfortunately, however, this tendency can fuel the addiction to suffering if what is familiar is a sense of victimhood, depression, blame, or some other negative state. In other words, your mind can *choose* unhappiness simply out of habit, in the same way you may reach for a familiar snack even when there are better options available. The first time you catch your mind doing this, it's a revelation!

A friend of mine went to stay at a beautiful tropical sanctuary filled with fruit trees and flowers. The land was owned by a small group of people who enjoyed the entire stretch of coastline to themselves. They had clean spring water to drink, wonderful organic food to eat, and beautiful surf breaking right outside their front door. Each person had plenty of space in which to live, and resources were so abundant that there was little to argue over. Still, it wasn't long before the members of this tiny community managed to find things around which they could create drama. "It's so sunny here every day; it never changes." "Did you see the mess he made with those coconut husks?" "She borrowed my bucket yesterday and didn't bring it back."

Most of us have experienced some version of this human tendency to seek out suffering, even when everything is fine. We get so used to surrounding ourselves with drama and sadness that when things are going well, we can't handle it for long and our minds look for problems. And if our minds can't find something real to suffer over, they will create something instead.

In this exercise, I invite you to observe your mind's addiction to suffering in action.

- The next time you notice your mind complaining, stop and ask yourself: "Is this really

something worth suffering over?" The mere act
of pausing and asking yourself that question
will disrupt the habitual cycle and give you the
space you need to establish a new pattern.

- Observe your thoughts and your body's reactions in as much detail as you can manage.
Imagine that you are a sports announcer,
narrating the action you see on the court.
"I'm feeling butterflies in my stomach. Now
my mind is saying I'm going to be late, and
my boss is going to be angry. Now it's saying
this is all Jennie's fault for asking me to help
her find her keys this morning. Now it's saying that I always let people walk all over me."

- Even as you distance yourself from your
thoughts, stay close to the sensations in
your body. Let them manifest like ripples
on a pond.

- Notice that, unlike your mental reactions,
these sensations can be harmless. If you let
them arise and pass away, they won't hurt you
or anyone else. They will not spread suffering.

When you attend to your emotions in this way, you maintain a state of personal freedom and break down your mind's addiction to suffering.

Exercise: Connecting with Healing

Sometimes the people we find most inspiring are the ones who have made the choice to heal their wounds. Think of the social workers and teachers who dedicated their lives to helping abused children after overcoming their own difficult childhoods, or the monks and nuns who survived war and went on to promote a message of peace. Although it wasn't necessarily easy for them to get over the pain of their pasts, their persistence benefited everyone around them. These inspiring people chose not only to heal their own wounds, but to use that healing in the service of others.

In this exercise, I invite you to connect with the energy of the people who inspire you, and draw strength from them to heal your own wounds.

- ◆ Call to mind a person who has overcome a serious inner wound like abuse, trauma, grief, or addiction. This can be a close friend or family member, or somebody you have never met, like a celebrity or spiritual teacher.

- Think of the qualities this person embodies—generosity, forgiveness, kindness, selflessness, maybe even a sense of humor.

- Generate these feelings in your own body, mind, and heart. What would it feel like to be as generous, forgiving, kind, selfless, and funny as the person you are imagining?

- Imagine this state of being in as much detail as possible. Notice how it affects your body, your mind, and your heart to imagine yourself possessing these qualities.

- Imagine the gifts you would be able to give your friends, family, and community if you embodied these qualities all the time. Perhaps you would be better able to comfort those who are suffering. Perhaps you would be less prone to spreading stress and anxiety, acting instead like a beacon of light. Imagine yourself being truly beneficial to everyone around you.

- Notice if your mind starts piping up with judgment, self-doubt, or negativity. "I'll never be as good as that person." "They're way more spiritual than I'll ever be." This is the voice of domestication attempting to pull you back into the addiction to suffering.

- Bring unconditional love to this voice, saying: "I hear you and I love you. I know you speak from old wounds, and I am holding you tight with love. The truth is, I *do* possess all these good qualities, and I have them inside me."

This exercise is extremely powerful because it allows you to experience the benefits of giving up your mind's addiction to suffering directly—which then becomes a strong motivation to continue the hard work. By connecting to the energy of people who have healed from wounds and overcome their own minds' addiction to suffering, you can more easily find the support to do so yourself.

Chapter 3

THE FREEDOM TO CHANGE

The shamans of my family have long taught that we humans are always wearing masks. Sometimes we wear them lightly, and sometimes they weigh on us very heavily indeed. In the Toltec tradition, these masks are not always considered a bad thing—sometimes they can be very useful. A skilled shaman can borrow masks as needed in order to interact with a particular person or group in the most effective and loving way. As long as you remember that it's just a mask, there's no problem.

For example, when you go to Thanksgiving dinner with your family, you may borrow the mask of "daughter" or "granddaughter" or "niece," instead of the mask of "shaman" or "team leader" or "boss." This doesn't mean that you repress these other selves or deny their existence. You just temporarily set them aside in favor of whatever mask serves the highest good of that moment and allows you to connect with the people around you in a loving and productive way.

Buddhists call the ability to wisely adapt your message to a specific person or audience *upaya*, or "skillful means." Think of how parents adapt their messages to their children as they grow up. The information they give a three-year-old will be very different from the information they give a seven-, or thirteen-, or twenty-one-year old. Skillful parents tailor each message to their children's ability to hear and understand it, and skillful shamans do the same thing. A skillful shaman is respectful of others' worldviews and does not seek to impress them, overwhelm them, or crack open their reality. Instead, a shaman always considers what is best and most appropriate for each person at a specific time.

When I am with certain apprentices or leading spiritual excursions to the pyramids in Teotihuacan, I often put on the mask of "teacher" and "guide." With other apprentices, I can shed the mask of "teacher," because it is no longer needed. When I'm at a barbecue in my neighborhood, I can happily wear the mask of "neighbor." If I showed up at the get-together in my "teacher" mask, it would be unskillful in the Buddhist sense of the word, because my neighbors aren't trying to connect with me in that capacity.

Managing your masks skillfully doesn't mean pandering to others or putting on whatever persona will make people like you. On the contrary, it means that you can bring your highest self to every encounter and express deep respect for every person you meet.

There's a wonderful story in the *Lotus Sutra* that illustrates the concept of skillful means. A man is at home with his three children when the house catches fire. He needs to get all three children safely out of the house, but they are absorbed in their games and don't want to go. To lure the children outside, he offers each one a different present. Because he pays attention to his children, he knows exactly what to offer them to pique their interest and get them to run to safety. In other words, he carefully tailors his message according to each child's needs, even though his ultimate goal remains the same—to get them all safely out of the burning house.

Just as the father in the story pays attention to his children's needs, in the Toltec tradition we always respect the needs and worldviews of the people around us. By managing our masks wisely, we bring our highest selves to all our interactions, even with those who are on a very different wavelength from us. Borrowing masks can help us build bridges with others and form connections where none might be possible otherwise. In this sense, masks can be very useful and beautiful.

The downside occurs when you confuse a particular mask with who you really are. When you identify with any mask, you assume a specific role or persona in a dream story, and these are always subject to the ups and downs of the dream world. But everything in the dream world ultimately collapses, so if you believe you *are* the mask, you will inevitably suffer when the mask is no longer useful to you or others. When you forget that any role you play is just a temporary mask, you have surrendered your freedom to change.

Changing Masks

A friend of mine was a tenured professor at a prestigious university on the East Coast. She taught computer science—about as cold and rational a field as you can get. When her sister was diagnosed with brain cancer, she took a sabbatical to take care of her. During the long hours she spent by her sister's bedside, she spent a lot of time reading spiritual books and meditating. One afternoon, she fell asleep and had a dream that she was carrying her sister on her back, walking her across a clear and sparkling stream to meet their Irish and Scottish ancestors who were waiting on the other side.

The next day, my friend held her sister's hand and sang to her as she took her last breaths. She felt that her dream had been a gift, allowing her to bring comfort and solace to her sister as she died. When she returned to the university the next semester, she continued to have dreams in which she assisted the souls of the dying to cross over. Although she had always been a skeptic who took "spiritual" matters with a grain of salt, she now found herself powerfully drawn to spiritual work. It wasn't long before she came to see herself as a shaman.

For a while, she tried to hide this from her colleagues. She didn't talk about her sister's death or what she was experiencing in her dreams. She even hid these feelings from her husband and her friends. When she brought home spiritual books from the library or bookstore, she hid them under the bed, only reading them when nobody else was home. She was afraid of what would happen if she gave herself the freedom to change. What would people say if they knew that she was now deeply interested in the very things she had disdained when she was younger? What would they do if she let them see this new side of her that was slowly but insistently coming out?

Not only that, but what would "real" shamans think if they heard that a middle-aged computer science professor was calling herself by that name? Surely, it was safer to stay in her assigned role. Otherwise she'd just upset everybody—both the colleagues who expected her to be logical and the "spiritual" people who had their own ideas about what a shaman should be.

As time went on, however, she came to feel that she was wearing a mask. When she went to work at the university, she could feel this mask obscuring her true self. It was only in rare moments that she felt safe taking it off. She began to realize that "computer science professor" had been a mask all along—it had just never bothered her before. That mask had allowed her to share her tremendous knowledge with talented students and to have an exciting and fulfilling career working with inspiring colleagues. It had given her a way to express her intelligence and take a deep dive into a field that fascinated her.

The problem arose when she came to assume that this mask was the *only* one available to her. She needed to give herself permission to don new masks to express her full self, but she was afraid of what would happen if people saw her in a different way. She hadn't yet figured out a graceful way to expand her range of masks. She hadn't yet found a graceful way to change.

Then one day, a colleague told her about a spiritual experience she had had while traveling in Mexico, and my friend realized that coming out as "spiritual" would not end her life or her career. She remembered that she only had one life to live, and it would be silly to waste it clinging to a single mask when there were other parts of herself that she wanted and needed to express. She told her colleague about the dreams she'd been having since her sister's death, and from then on, she began to integrate her spiritual self with her identity as a college professor.

She claimed the freedom to change.

Saying "No"

Claiming the freedom to change means embracing another freedom—the freedom to say "no." From the moment you are born, you become a character in other peoples' dreams. The doctor says: "It's a girl!" And right away, your parents start imagining a particular future for you, starting with a pink room and working their way up to a specific career and romantic partner. Or the doctor says: "It's a boy!" And they immediately imagine a different future entirely.

How is it possible that these two words—*girl* and *boy*—cast such a powerful spell? Yet for almost all of us, these words shape the first dream that is thrust upon us. They define the first agreement we learn to accept, without even realizing we're accepting it. The dream of binary gender is so widespread, and so powerful, that it is only in recent decades that our society has begun to acknowledge its limitations, or to accept the people who refuse to be bound by it.

As we grow up, the adults around us cast more and more magic spells, enmeshing us in more and more agreements. Perhaps you were told you were Catholic, so you had to follow certain rules. Or you may have been told that, because you're good at math, you should become an engineer.

Then there are the unspoken agreements. "All the men in our family become alcoholics, and you likely will too." "All the women in our family develop eating disorders, and you likely will too." "Our people don't associate with people from *that* group." This is domestication in action. We learn that if we accept these agreements, we receive approval from the people around us. If we don't—if we dare to consider change—we risk being shamed or rejected.

But when you are called to change, you must summon the courage to decline these old agreements, even if you fear that doing so will upset or disappoint others. You must have the courage to say "no."

A friend of mine had been married to her high school sweetheart for almost twenty years. She and her husband were regarded as an institution by their friends—a nearly unheard-of success story in a world where divorce is common. Near-strangers approached her for relationship advice. The whole world seemed to share in the dream that she and her husband were the ideal couple, destined to be together for life. She heard so many stories about how lucky she was to be in such a long-lasting and apparently loving relationship that she felt it was her duty to uphold this dream for her friends, her family, and the world at large, despite the many problems that were developing in the marriage. She did not feel that she had the freedom to change this dream, even as her husband became abusive. She had lost the power to say "no."

Then one day, she found a lump in her breast and, as she waited for the test results to come back, she realized that she only had one chance to live her life. Nobody was coming to save her from her marriage. She was the only person who could break the old agreements that were keeping her there—agreements about loyalty, commitment, and making things work at all costs. She was the only person who could listen politely to the stories other people told her about her wonderful marriage, and say: "Actually, I am making a different choice now."

When my friend finally left her marriage, some refused to understand her position. After all, she had become a character in *their* dreams about what a beautiful marriage looked like. Going against their scripts upset them, because it contradicted all the stories they'd put so much artistry into creating. At the same time, my friend's life became much better, because she was finally creating her own artwork. Instead of suffering on the inside while playing out other peoples' dreams, she decided to change her agreement, and her life got better as a result.

Once we realize that other people are all dreaming, it becomes much easier to have compassion for them instead of being annoyed when they try to assign us roles in their dreams.

The Art of Shapeshifting

In my family's Toltec tradition, we teach the art of shapeshifting. I'm not talking about turning yourself into a black cat or a jaguar. I'm talking about living in dynamic relationship to life—being responsive to circumstances and loosening your grip on any single identity. Shamans understand that the masks of teacher, student, worker, victim, victor, and even man and woman are expressions of one aspect of our selves, not complete and final descriptions. Although it may be appropriate to take on the identity of teacher or student or even victim in certain situations—in the same way that it can be appropriate to dress a certain way depending on whether you are going to a wedding or a rock concert—shamans never lose touch with the fact that these identities are temporary and changeable.

This freedom to change is perhaps the defining characteristic of youth. Children and teenagers are often more in touch with their shapeshifting powers than adults. Think of the way children play dress-up, joyfully turning themselves into cowboys one day and princesses the next. Or the way teenagers may identify as punk rockers one year and as athletes the next, or as goths one year and as environmental activists the next. When we are young, we latch on to a certain identity with great intensity and vigor, only to discard it when the next identity catches our fancy. We don't waste energy clinging to old identities, but allow ourselves to transform as the spirit moves us.

As we grow older, however, we are often told that we should stop changing. We are told we should choose a career, or a spiritual path, or a spouse, or a specific role in our family, and stick to it. In modern society, changing one of these roles can sometimes even be associated with failure or shame. We are often afraid to let people know that we are getting divorced, or going by different pronouns, or embarking on a different spiritual path than the one in which we were raised, because we have been taught to believe that such changes mean that we have failed or broken some unwritten contract with the people around us.

The people in your church may expect you to remain a part of the congregation for life, and you fear that they will experience your changing paths as a betrayal. Or maybe your parents are expecting grandchildren, and you know they will be disappointed if you separate from your spouse. There can be a lot of pressure to stay on one track, and this can make it scary to make the changes you need. Think of the suffering my professor friend went through because she feared the consequences of "shapeshifting" into a new role as shaman.

But when you surrender your freedom to change, you simultaneously surrender your ability to create. You become locked in a narrow, rigid identity and become blind to the infinite possibilities of life. For example, if you identify as a workaholic, you may lose touch with the side of yourself that is playful, relaxed, and at ease.

If you identify as a philanderer, you may never discover your potential for deep commitment and devoted love. If you identify as a lone wolf, you may inadvertently cut off your capacity for friendship and your talent for community building. Instead of creating the artwork of your life from a rich palette of colors, you may start to limit yourself in both conscious and unconscious ways. And this limitation doesn't only impact you—it prevents you from fully developing the gifts you can offer to others.

My professor friend now offers shamanic services to close friends—a gift that would never have had the chance to flower if she hadn't given herself permission to change. Other friends of mine who have changed careers, left relationships, and transitioned from one gender identity to another have all brought incredible gifts to the world because of those changes—gifts that would have been stifled forever if they had remained in their old roles.

The Lesson of Siddhartha

Hermann Hesse's classic novel *Siddhartha* contains a beautiful anecdote about shapeshifting. In the final pages of the book, Siddhartha's friend Govinda finds him sitting by a river. Siddhartha has been searching for enlightenment by following various teachers and trying on various identities. After spending years living as a prince, an ascetic, a businessman, and a seeker, he has finally found enlightenment while meditating beside the river. Siddhartha invites Govinda to kiss him on the forehead, and when Govinda does so, this is what happens:

He no longer saw the face of his friend Siddhartha, instead he saw other faces, many, a long sequence, a flowing river of faces, of hundreds, of thousands, which all came and disappeared, and yet all seemed to be there simultaneously, which all constantly changed and renewed themselves, and which were still all Siddhartha.

From a shamanic perspective, we could say that Siddhartha had transcended his limited identity as a prince, an ascetic, a seeker, and a businessman, and instead become a shapeshifter—one who is in a constant state of change and renewal. Govinda literally sees all these masks flowing past him in the river, beautiful and ephemeral—each one an expression of the infinite life force flowing through Siddhartha himself.

In other stories, Siddhartha confronts a demonic being called Mara who attempts to trick him into latching on to a single, limited identity and therefore to remain in a cycle of suffering. By resisting Mara's tricks, Siddhartha realizes that his identity is limitless and ever changing, and he avoids getting trapped by the addiction to suffering.

Just like Siddhartha, we are all subject to the constant temptation to identify with one or more limited versions of ourselves. This temptation can take many forms. Perhaps our partners, or parents, or children need to see us in a certain way, so we take on that identity to please them. Or we place a high value on a certain identity and cling to it to please ourselves. Or we simply get so used to seeing ourselves in a certain way that we lose touch with our limitless nature. Whatever the cause, we become trapped in a fixed identity and give up our freedom to change.

We've all been asked questions that seek to fix our identity in some way. "What are you?" "What is your profession?" "What race are you?" "What kind of person are you?" When I'm asked these questions, I think to myself: "I'm just life." I am infinite potential manifesting in a specific form at a specific moment; nothing more and nothing less. I no longer commit to labels as I did when I was younger. Although I may still say I'm a rock fan, or a Toltec warrior, or a dog lover, I speak these words for the benefit of the listener only, as I'm always aware of the vastness behind these temporary masks.

Resisting Change

Shamans place a high value on their freedom to change, but they also extend this freedom to others. And sometimes this is even harder than extending this freedom to yourself. If you are used to someone playing a certain role or wearing a particular mask in your own story, you may become angry, frightened, or defensive when that person expresses a need to change.

A friend of mine felt very anxious when his wife gave up her high-paying corporate job to work at a non-profit organization. Not only did this have a big impact on the family finances, but it also profoundly challenged his conception of who she was—and by extension, who he was. He reacted to this perceived threat by pressuring her to go back to her old job. He even hid this change from friends out of fear that it would affect their social standing. It was only after some deep soul-searching that he realized that he was holding on to an identity that was preventing growth for both his wife and himself.

Our resistance to change can also derive from the mind's addiction to suffering. Another friend of mine spent many years holding anger toward his father, an alcoholic who had abandoned his family when he was a child. When my friend was in his thirties, his father re-established contact and tried to make amends. He had gotten treatment for his alcoholism and was highly involved in community service and spiritual work.

This was a very positive change from the moody, disconnected person the man had been before. Yet my friend was so attached to a negative image of his father that, for years, he resisted and even resented this positive change. He had become attached to the identity he had created around his childhood abandonment.

He was addicted to the suffering he experienced when he told himself and others this story throughout the years. Consequently, he wasn't about to give up this story without a fight!

Finally, a friend took him aside and told him that his own father had died recently after a long illness. Although this person had not been close with his father when he was a child either, they had gotten to know each other well as adults. And he was forever grateful for the time they spent together. The role of "parent to a young child" was not one in which his father had thrived, but he did surprisingly well as "parent of an adult." He implied that the same might be true for my friend.

Indeed, when my friend took the courageous step of giving his own father a second chance, he realized that he could give much more now, in the present, than he had been able to give all those years ago. By allowing his father to change, he finally received the love that had been inaccessible to him as a child—and this caused my friend to change too.

When we deny other people the freedom to change, we stifle the flow of life, blocking off powerful currents of love, forgiveness, and joy. Shamans honor the freedom to change in both themselves and others, and recognize that change is the defining characteristic of life.

Exercise: Wearing Your Masks Lightly

In this exercise, I invite you to create some space around the masks you wear on a regular basis.

- Write down a list of every identity that applies to you. "I am a woman." "I am a mother." "I am a cancer survivor." "I am a best friend." "I am a yogi." "I am a massage therapist." "I am depressed."

- Go through your list and turn every statement into a question. "Am I a woman?" "Am I a cancer survivor?" "Am I a depressed person?" "Am I a massage therapist?"

- Ask yourself these questions and pay attention to any subtle changes in your body and emotions. Do you experience a feeling of lightness in your body when you question whether you are truly a woman? A depressed person? A career person? Do you experience a feeling of expansion or contraction? Do you want to laugh? Cry? Get angry?

When one person I know did this exercise, she noticed a feeling of tightness and sadness when she asked herself: "Am I a wife?" She had never realized how unhappy she was in her marriage, which was very traditional in its division of labor. After sitting with these feelings for a while, she made the decision to go back to school for a business degree and forge a career for herself that would give her an identity outside of "only" being a wife.

The emotions and sensations you feel when you do this exercise will give you important information about the areas in which you are denying yourself the freedom to change, and thereby limiting your personal freedom. By turning your identity statements into questions, you learn to wear your masks lightly. By listening to the subtle answers provided by your mind and body, you get in touch with your infinite potential to change, whether or not you feel called to act on that potential at this moment.

Think of the way you would hold a baby bird you found in the grass—gently, with cupped hands, giving it the freedom to fly away when the time is right. By holding your many identities in the same way, you can make wise and skillful use of all of them for the time that they are with you, while leaving yourself open to change.

Exercise: Acknowledging the Gifts of Change

Many of us experience an involuntary wave of resistance when we are confronted with change, before we even take the time to think about whether the change may be positive. This resistance can take the form of physical reactions like clenching, sweating, or shallow breathing. Or it may manifest as mental reactions like anxious thoughts and predictions, or as emotional reactions like fear, sadness, or anger. These reactions can feel so uncomfortable that we can often make the mistake of believing they are "proof" the change in question is bad. Yet often, the very changes that make us the most anxious end up being the most positive ones for our lives.

In this exercise, I invite you to forge a new relationship with your own natural resistance to change.

◆ Look back over your life and write down a list of the changes that scared you the most. This can include simple things like starting kindergarten, or more complex things like changing careers, getting married, becoming a parent, or letting go of an addiction.

◆ Write down the physical, mental, and emotional symptoms you experienced as you contemplated these changes. For example, perhaps you experienced insomnia, worry, and looping thoughts as you questioned whether you would be able to take good care of a baby.

◆ Consider your *current* relationship to this event. In the long run, was this change as bad as you feared? What unexpected gifts and benefits did you receive as a result of this change? Write these down.

◆ For every change you listed, write down the greatest fear you experienced about it, and the greatest benefit you received from it. "Although I feared that becoming a parent would bring out the worst in me, I discovered an immense capacity to love." "Although I feared that I'd never be close to anyone again after my best friend died, her death made me value my relationships even more highly, and I now have a very tight circle of friends."

This exercise can help you develop the awareness that your initial resistance to a particular change is not necessarily an accurate reflection of your long-term feelings about it. Sometimes the changes we fear the most bring us the greatest gifts. The more you learn to recognize and appreciate this paradox, the easier it will be for you to embrace change.

Chapter 4

THE FREEDOM TO FEEL

In the Toltec tradition, we believe that just as we have a physical body that feels heat and cold, hunger and sleepiness, we also have an emotional body that is beautifully designed to feel sadness, and joy, and everything in between. Most of us have at least a basic connection to our physical bodies—we put on a sweater when we feel cold and eat when we feel hungry. But when it comes to our emotional bodies, many of us don't offer ourselves the same support. In fact, in many cases, we have been taught to ignore our emotional bodies, or even to hate and suppress our own emotions.

For some of us, this suppression may be so automatic that we don't even realize it's happening. It just feels "normal" to tamp down our emotions, and we accept the consequences and side-effects of this suppression as "normal" as well—frustration, discomfort, an inability to form close connections with others, and a tendency to erupt or melt down when the pressure builds too much. We spend our precious life force in the service of *suppressing* our emotional body—a strange situation indeed!

Imagine visiting a country in which it was considered shameful to breathe. Inhabitants of this strange place go to great lengths to conceal the fact that they are breathing—holding their bodies rigid to prevent their chests from rising and falling, trying to muffle the sound of air passing through their nostrils, and other strange behaviors. As a visitor to this culture, it is probably obvious to you that suppressing the normal and healthy flow of breath is a crazy thing to do. After all, *everybody* breathes—why pretend otherwise?

You may also notice that the people here have developed some pretty painful mental and physical health problems because of their obsession with hiding and suppressing their breath. For example, they may have heightened anxiety as a result of restricting the flow of oxygen to their brains. They may lash out in anger and despair when their frustration becomes too intense. They may get frequent headaches. In some cases, their skin may even turn blue. Wouldn't you be tempted to say: "You guys are crazy! Breathing is good and natural, not bad or shameful. Please just let yourselves breathe."

Yet if citizens of this strange culture came to visit *our* country, they would probably say something quite similar to us. They might look at the way we hide and suppress our emotions, and say: "You guys are crazy! Feeling is good and natural, not bad or shameful. Please just let yourselves feel."

I have a friend who had been taught from childhood that it wasn't safe to show her emotions, or even to feel them. As an adult, her husband complained that she always denied feeling sad or worried, even when it was obvious to him that she was experiencing those emotions. As for my friend, she grew defensive, telling him that he was projecting his own feelings onto her. They usually ended up arguing over who was "really" having which emotions! It was only after years of inner work that my friend felt safe enough to acknowledge when she was feeling scared, vulnerable, or sad, and to feel those emotions completely.

When my friend finally started feeling her emotions, something incredible happened. Other parts of her life that had been blocked or stuck began to flow again. Her relationships with her parents and her husband began to evolve, and her chronic back pain began to fade away. She felt stronger, more capable, and better equipped to face the challenges of life. Instead of being weakened by her emotions, they acted as a powerful catalyst, setting her on a path of personal freedom.

Feel to Heal

Feelings can be powerful medicine. Just like other forms of medicine, however, they can sometimes cause discomfort. For the magic to work, you may need to tolerate a little sting, a little bitterness, or some other sensation you may at first identify as unpleasant. If you've ever been treated with acupuncture or swallowed a spoonful of hot ginger with cayenne for a cold, you know exactly what I'm talking about.

The same is true of your emotions. At first, you may avoid them because you feel skittish about the possible discomfort you may feel. But as you progress down the path to personal freedom, you may be surprised to discover that you start to welcome these uncomfortable sensations.

A woman I know who loved to swim balked at jumping into the cold water of the river near her home. She hovered on the bank, grimacing and hesitating, dragging out the process of getting in the water, even though she enjoyed swimming and knew that it was good for her health. But she soon realized that every time she went for a swim, she came out feeling happy, energized, and filled with strength. After a month or two, she stopped fighting the sensation of the cold water, In fact, she began to crave it, because she had learned to associate it with all the positive feelings that came shortly thereafter.

Although many of us shy away from the "cold water" of difficult emotions, when we learn to lean into them, we find that the discomfort they bring initially also has tremendous healing power wrapped up inside it.

In the Toltec tradition, we cultivate the courage to feel *all* our emotions, including the ones we think of as unpleasant, because we know that they are invitations to finding our own personal freedom. These emotions are the ones that can show us where we may need to forgive ourselves or others, or let go of rigid ideas about how things should or shouldn't be. They may also invite us to look more deeply at any story we believe about ourselves. They may help us to see what's possible for us, and show us if we are clinging to a particular mask too tightly.

The Power of Stories

Most of us have a habit of immediately converting our emotions into stories. When it comes to so-called "negative" emotions, the stories we create tend to feed our mind's addiction to suffering. When a friend confides that he is sad and disappointed because he learned that his significant other has been unfaithful, most of us feel a twinge of sadness in our emotional bodies for his sake. But in many cases, we don't stop at feeling empathy. Instead, we start thinking about the ways in which we, too, have been hurt by the people around us. We call up stories of our own experiences of betrayal, and before we know it, we're suffering too.

In this example, the cause of the emotion and subsequent story are easy to trace, but that isn't always the case. Think of the last time you felt a little bit down. Did you stay with the feeling in its pure form, considering how it felt in your body? Or did you immediately try to figure out *why*, exactly, you were feeling that way? If, like many people, you went looking for a reason, I'm going to guess that it wasn't long before you found one—or several.

After a little bit of searching, your mind identifies a cause or set of causes for your emotional state—the weather, or a thoughtless remark by someone you interacted with that day—and before you know it, you've crafted an elaborate story explaining how this emotion came into existence, and what must be done to make it go away.

Before long, your story grows legs and starts to take on a life of its own. You realize it's not just the weather and the thoughtless remark that made you sad; it's your failure to excel at your job, which was in turn caused by your parents' failure to give you adequate encouragement when you were a child. Soon, your entire *life* starts to feel like a reason to feel sad. Your story becomes a trellis on which sadness can spread out like a vine in all directions, taking up far more space than the original, pure emotion. This is how the mind uses stories to feed its addiction to suffering. Eventually, you forget that your story is just that—a story. And you surrender your personal freedom the moment you do so.

The first step in reclaiming your personal freedom is to notice when you're telling yourself a story. This is easier said than done, however. After all, most of us have been telling ourselves these kinds of stories ever since we learned enough language to think. The mind's storytelling habit can feel as natural as breathing. But just as we can train ourselves to notice our breathing, we can also train ourselves to notice when we have begun to tell a story.

Start by watching your mind for thoughts that attempt to explain what you are feeling. While these attempts may feel reasonable and useful, it's like dragging the ocean floor with a net—you're going to scrape up a lot of things you weren't looking for, in addition to that one particular fish you were trying to catch. Before you know it, you're not just feeling the emotions you are experiencing right now; you're also associating them with past events and speculating on how this may affect your future. Suddenly, you've moved out of the present moment into remembrance, projection, fantasy, and conjecture.

Instead, try to pause and take a break the moment you catch yourself telling a story about your emotions. Tell yourself: "This is a story." Then, conduct a scan of your body. Notice what you are feeling in your muscles, your bones, your stomach, and your heart. Imagine you have no access to language whatsoever, and you can *only* experience your emotions physically, with no mental component. When you become practiced at this, you can begin to experience pure emotions, instead of the muddy, story-fed versions most of us are used to.

When you learn to feel your emotions in a pure way, you experience them at "actual size"—neither inflating them and giving them room to spread, nor artificially shrinking them and trying to make them go away. This doesn't mean that you should push down past memories or trauma. Those certainly need to be dealt with, and I have included an exercise at the end of this chapter to help you do that. But by experiencing your emotions at actual size, you can maintain your personal freedom instead of getting dragged into the fog of regret for the past or fears for the future. You can stay rooted in the awareness that you are the nagual, the life force, not any particular emotion you are experiencing in the moment or any story that your mind may generate as a result.

Feeling vs. Reacting

Although *feeling* your emotions is a beautiful and healthy way to live, be careful not to *react* to them. Some of us have been domesticated to the idea that feeling our emotions means yelling, lashing out, or otherwise "losing control." Depending on your family environment, you may even have grown up believing that you have no choice but to "lose control" if you let yourself feel a strong emotion, and it can come as a surprise to hear that emotions and reactions are in fact two separate things.

I can relate to this because, when I was younger, I tended to lash out at others when I felt threatened, neglected, or ashamed. When I started to experience those uncomfortable feelings, *bam*, I found a way to discharge them by starting an argument. My grandmother told me that I was like a baby rattlesnake—more dangerous than an adult snake, because it hasn't yet learned to control its poison. Unlike adult snakes, who preserve their venom for dire emergencies, baby rattlers strike at the slightest provocation. You can imagine how much chaos I sowed during my baby-rattlesnake phase, hurting myself and others with my outbursts. It was only after careful practice that I learned to control my own poison.

By controlling my poison, however, I don't mean that I stopped feeling my emotions. In fact, quite the opposite. To become an adult rattlesnake, I had to learn to feel my emotions completely, instead of escaping into a mental story and lashing out in reaction.

When you lash out at others, you may believe that what you are doing is feeling when, in fact, you are reacting. If you've been taught since childhood that feeling and reacting are one and the same, it can take some time to get used to the idea that they are actually two entirely separate responses.

Exercise: Toltec Inventory and Recapitulation

Sometimes the emotions you most need to feel and process are old ones, like grief or anger you've been suppressing for years. You may not have had the skill or resources to work with these emotions when they first occurred, and they may have been living inside you all this time, waiting for their energy to be released. This exercise can help you go back and consciously clear these difficult emotions, freeing up their energy at last.

In the Toltec tradition, we have two powerful tools to help us forgive and release any emotional poison we are carrying around from past experiences—the Toltec inventory and recapitulation. The first is a thorough review of the major events of your life, especially those that were traumatic; the second is a breathing exercise that helps you release any negativity you uncover as you review these memories and reclaim your emotional power. These two tools work together to help you resolve any pain you are still carrying around because of old wounds. I used these practices extensively to process the traumatic experiences I lived through, and I continue to use them today.

A complete Toltec inventory involves reviewing the major events of your entire life. To begin, however, choose just one memory or experience that still causes you pain. This may be a memory of a time when someone hurt you, or a time when you made a mistake that still fills you with guilt and regret. Choose an experience with which you still struggle and around which you would like to find lasting peace.

- Write down everything you can remember about the traumatic experience. Make a complete inventory of the memory, the way you would inventory the groceries in your kitchen or the tools in your workshop. Leave no shelf or drawer unexamined. This may bring up intense emotions or even physical sensations, but the act of writing it all down will ultimately help to diminish their intensity.

- Nobody needs to see what you write except you. You can delete the text from your computer when you are finished, or burn the piece of paper if you are writing by hand.

- Write down not only as many details as possible about what happened, but also how you felt about the event, how you reacted, and anything else you can call to mind.

Once you have completed your inventory, you are ready to move on to the recapitulation practice.

Recapitulation is a process by which you can remove the emotional charge of negative experiences that you have been holding on to so that you can reintegrate them. Think of a string of Christmas lights. When they're plugged in, they light up and may even feel warm to the touch. But when you unplug them, they become cold and inert—in other words, neutral. Likewise, when you "unplug" your negative experiences from their emotional charge, they become neutral and can no longer hurt or distract you.

Recapitulation uses the power of the breath to cleanse the negative emotions from your traumatic memory. When you inhale, you draw back all the energy you've invested in this memory; when you exhale, you expel all the negativity you've taken on because of the event.

- Sit or lie in a comfortable place where you won't be disturbed for several minutes.

- Reflect on the traumatic event you wrote about in the Toltec inventory, but now focus on the feelings you had during the experience.

- Inhale deeply, calling back all the negative emotions you experienced during the event. Emotions are just energy. By taking this energy back, you can cleanse it of its negative charge and put it to better use somewhere else.

- As your breath enters your lungs, imagine this trapped energy returning to your body. This energy belongs to *you*, and you get to decide what to do with it.

- Still thinking about the traumatic event, begin to exhale. As you do so, imagine yourself expelling the negative emotions you feel toward the memory. Push out all the shame, anger, guilt, or sadness tied up with it. These emotions cannot hurt you any longer. They are not yours anymore.

- Reflect on the memory as you inhale and exhale. Imagine the energy that was trapped

in it being released, cleansed, and restored
to you for higher purposes.

◆ Breathe in and out until you feel that the
negative energy has been eliminated, decon-
taminated, and returned to you in a pure and
useful form.

Don't worry if you cannot fully neutralize a traumatic memory in one session. It can take several ses-
sions to clear an event completely.

Every time you use these two practices, you will
find that the traumatic memory feels a little bit less
charged. Over time, the sense of pain and activation
you experience around it will continue to diminish,
until it no longer has the capacity to flood you with
overwhelming emotions. You'll know your energy has
been fully reclaimed when you can think and even
talk about the experience without feeling any negative
charge coming up as you do so.

Exercise: Shifting Your Perspective

Another way to drain the emotional charge from traumatic memories is to shift your perspective from the

role of victim to the role of experiencer. While it may be true that you were a victim in many of these situations, shifting your perspective can help you drain the emotional poison from an experience and reclaim your role as the artist of your life.

- In your journal, make a list of some of the difficult experiences in your life.

- Rewrite your list, reframing them as learning experiences. For example, rephrase "I got mugged walking home from the subway" as "I got to experience what it was like to get mugged." Rephrase "My girlfriend dumped me" as "I got to find out what heartbreak feels like."

- Notice when you think or talk about these experiences whether you can use the same language. In this way, you shift your perspective from that of victim to the more positive perspective of someone in control of the event.

You can also try seeing your wounds from the perspective of someone who has already healed from them.

- In your journal, write down a list of your old stories—the ones you most frequently tell yourself and others about your life. "I have an anxiety disorder." "My first big relationship ended badly and shattered my ability to trust."

- For each item on your list, add a positive statement that shows you are healing from that wound. "With every passing day I am developing a healthier relationship with my anxious thoughts and feelings." "With every passing day I am rebuilding my ability to relate with others and finding more and more reasons to trust in life."

Shifting the emphasis in this way affirms your capacity to heal, and turns down the volume on the intense emotions associated with the experience. This makes you aware of the fact that life is a process. Your life didn't stop the moment you were wounded; instead, it continues to unfold in beautiful ways.

Realizing that you don't need to suffer from your wounds for the rest of your life can help you to forgive the people who have harmed you—including yourself. As you heal from your wounds, the desire to blame and punish fades away, and you can reclaim all the energy that was going into those processes for a higher purpose.

Chapter 5

THE FREEDOM TO SEE

The shamans of my family teach that we have been given the gift of a human body on the physical plane in order to learn how to love ourselves and others, but that many of us are blinded by distractions. We fall victim to the lie that we are somehow separate from the nagual—the life force that is inside all of us in equal measure. We are scared off by our internal demons, and forget that they are only projections of ourselves. Worst of all, we only see what we want to see, and mistake that limited perception for all of reality.

I learned this lesson myself in 2001, when I went to the dentist for a root canal. At first, everything seemed to go as planned and the procedure seemed routine. But as I was driving home, I began to feel a strange pain in my eyes. It hurt to look to the left or right. After a few minutes, it even began to hurt to look straight ahead. When I got home, I decided to take a nap in the hopes that I would feel better, but when I woke up, the pain in my eyes was even worse—and I was completely blind.

Panicked, I called to my ex-wife and told her I couldn't see. She phoned my dad, who instructed her to take me immediately to see my aunt, who is an eye doctor. As we sped down the highway, the pressure in my head kept building, until it felt as if my skull would explode. I spent the drive bent over with my head between my knees, trying anything I could think of to reduce the pain.

After examining my eyes, my aunt said that I might never see again. During my years of drug use, I'd done damage to my optic nerve and, when the dentist injected the anesthesia to perform the root canal, she'd unknowingly triggered a massive swelling behind my eyes. My ex-wife and aunt took me to the hospital, where doctors admitted me and gave me more anesthetic, which sank me into a deep meditation.

In this state, I traveled to a place far beyond sound and sight. When I woke up, my family members had come from all over to be with me. I could feel their presence as they stood around me. I couldn't see them, but I could hear their voices, which were filled with fear and worry. Yet suddenly, I felt at peace. I knew I could either choose to suffer from this experience, or I could embrace it as a learning opportunity and a gift. Even though I was the one who had gone blind, I ended up comforting my family, reassuring them that everything was going to be okay. I knew that, even if I were blind, the only person who could turn my personal heaven into a hell was *me*.

My whole life, I've always loved the experience of gazing deeply into another person's eyes. I'm fascinated by the way eyes can communicate at a level that goes beyond words, so that two people meeting for the first time can come to know each other instantly, just through eye contact. In my friendships and relationships, I've always experienced the most potent connection in the form of eye contact. But as I lay in that hospital bed, I began to let go of my attachment to eyesight. I knew I could still connect with people through my sense of touch, my voice, and my inner knowing.

I was completely blind for about three weeks. I spent a lot of this time lucid dreaming—an ability I'd never had before. Lucid dreaming is the ability to "wake up" inside a dream and become an active participant instead of a passive observer. In one such dream, I was walking in the desert when I stumbled upon a cave that was filled with human souls, with demons guarding them and holding them prisoner. But the demons didn't scare me, because I knew that if they hurt me, I could just fly into the sun, where I would be joined with the infinite. So I encouraged the other souls to fly into the sun as well.

When I did, a large, aggressive demon approached and loomed over me, staring down at me with fiery eyes.

"How dare you take away my prisoners and send them into the sun!" he scolded.

"How can you keep them in a cave?" I shot back. "They belong to the sun, and I belong to the sun, and so do you."

The demon laughed contemptuously, then leaped forward to attack me. I wrapped my arms around him and said: "I forgive you."

As I held the demon close, I could see all my former selves floating past, making their way to the sun. I saw myself as a child, as a teenager, as a young adult, and finally as myself at my current age. "Thanks for coming back for us," these former selves said. As they floated past, they gazed at me in total forgiveness, forgiving me for the harm I had caused them when I was unaware.

Three days after this dream, my eyesight returned. I woke up one morning, and suddenly I could see the light flooding into my hospital room. I could see my hands and the faces of my family. I was filled with love and gratitude. It seemed to me that my period of blindness had been an incredible gift. It had forced me to go deep within myself, seeing with my inner vision instead of my eyes. With this inner vision, I could finally see the ways in which I needed to forgive myself, and the ways in which I'd been blind.

Flying Blind

We all have areas of our lives in which we have made unconscious agreements to remain blind to certain things, refusing to see events or situations for what they are. In my own life, this manifested as the choice to see myself as a victim, instead of seeing all the ways in which I was creating my own problems. Before my experience with physical blindness, I only saw myself as a prisoner of the cave demon. I didn't see that I also had the power to free myself from the cave. I only saw the ways in which other people were hurting me or keeping me down, and was blind to the ways in which they were supporting and uplifting me. I was convinced that if I allowed myself to realize how other people were supporting me, I would no longer be able to claim the role of victim—so I made sure that I never let myself *see*.

I am not alone in this. A friend of mine had an unconscious agreement that she was a failure. Although she'd achieved many things that others only dreamed of, she could only see the ways in which she'd fallen short and remained blind to all her successes. When she got an e-mail praising her for her work, her eyes glazed over—she *literally* couldn't let herself see the complimentary words!

Another friend lived in a beautiful home, but could only see the minor flaws—a single dirty glass in the sink, a house plant with a few brown leaves that hadn't been watered. While guests exclaimed over his beautiful home, all he could see was the mess.

We all place filters on our perceptions that control the things we choose to see, or refuse to see. These filters are often there to feed the mind's addiction to suffering. They create a form of blindness in which we stop seeing the whole of reality, and only see a cramped and distorted slice of it. Instead of seeing the complex and infinitely beautiful dance of life, we see only our own stories.

This refusal to see constitutes the primary way in which we perpetuate our addiction to suffering. We become very adept at seeing the things that hurt us, while tuning out the truths that could make us happy. But when you realize the ways in which you are using your own perceptions to go against yourself, you can uplift yourself with your power of vision. When you discover that you are the love of your life, you immediately begin to see life through the eyes of love. Everywhere you go, you can look for the beauty, the peace, and the divinity in all things and in all situations. And when you do that, you start radiating beauty, peace, and divinity to all people.

Learning to See

If you are not in the habit of seeing the divinity in all things, you can start by making a simple request within your own mind: "Show me the divinity in this moment." Whether you're taking a walk in the forest, or trapped in a stressful meeting, or lying in a hospital bed, you can always make this request: "Please show me the divinity that exists right here, right now." And the simple act of *asking* to see beauty can change your life. You begin to see everything that exists as part of the Divine Mother. Even the negative experiences in your life are part of this divinity. They were supposed to happen, and they are perfect as well. Every experience that you have is perfect.

When you say that something wasn't supposed to happen, or that something is supposed to be different somehow, you're simply not seeing life clearly. Everything is perfect. It's only when you surrender to a situation or circumstance—going blind, or losing your lover, or some other trauma—that you really begin to understand and appreciate life. That's when you start to become one with life, instead of fighting against it. That's when you stop flying blind and begin to *see*.

Once you realize how distorted your perceptions are, you can never go back to seeing life in the same way. When you banish your self-imposed suffering, you can really begin to live. As Siddhartha cries out when he wakes up to become the Buddha and realizes that the person creating his suffering has been *him* all along:

> Oh housebuilder! Now you are seen. You shall
> not build a house again for me. All your beams
> are broken, the ridgepole is shattered. The
> mind has become freed from conditioning:
> the end of craving has been reached.

When you learn to see, you are just like the Buddha, declining to build any more houses of suffering in which to reside, choosing instead to live out under the open sky.

The dwellings we build for ourselves when we limit our perceptions are constraining. They have ceilings and walls. They delineate a certain space that we can easily mistake for the whole of reality. When we tear down these dwellings, breaking the beams and shattering the ridgepoles, we enter a much larger reality in which our old habits of suffering simply can't exist. Once we see ourselves as part of the Divine, our old "houses" look shabby and small. And we can't go back inside, even if we want to.

Doing Your Best to Perceive Divinity Everywhere

Although many of us are familiar with the concept of doing our best when it comes to concrete actions like doing our job at work, taking a math test, or competing in a sport, we can also bring the best of ourselves to our perceptions of reality.

Can you do your best to see the divinity in all things, even when you are feeling tired, frustrated, defeated, or overwhelmed? Can you do your best to see through your own stories to the larger truth that lies beyond them? Can you do your best to notice when you have a blind spot, and gently invite yourself to see the things you couldn't see before?

When a woman I know went on a camping trip, she was annoyed to discover that some nearby campers were noisy partiers. She had gone to the forest for peace and quiet, but all she could hear was their beer bottles clinking and the sound of their noisy laughter as they tuned their guitars. As she lay in her tent trying to read, feeling more and more irritated by her "thoughtless" neighbors, she entered a truly miserable state. Then, a few minutes later, one of the noisy group showed up outside her tent and invited her to join them for a campfire.

It turned out that one of the people in the group had terminal cancer, and all of his old friends had gotten together to take him on one last camping trip. The behavior that my friend had perceived as thoughtless and boorish was actually a deeply meaningful ritual for those involved. As she sat by the campfire enjoying the music and the deep currents of love running between the old friends, she perceived the divinity in the people she had written off as losers just minutes before. She began to see the best in them instead of the worst, and her personal hell transformed into a heaven.

Just as we try to do our best in our concrete actions—like performing at work, or taking a math test, or competing in a sport—we can also bring the best of ourselves to our perceptions of others and of reality.

Exercise: Seeing Through the Eyes of Love

Learning to see the world through the eyes of love can help you to awaken to the divinity in all things. This exercise offers a simple practice to help you do that.

- Go for a walk on a familiar street in your neighborhood or in a crowded downtown area.

- As you walk along, imagine that you are God, looking at the world through the eyes of infinite tenderness.

- Look at the people around you. Do they seem more beautiful than usual? Do you feel more compassion for them?

- Notice how the quality of your mind changes when you look at the world through the eyes of love. Do you create the same running commentary? Do you make the same criticisms of reality? Or do you see everything as being perfect the way it is?

- Practice looking at the world through these eyes for a longer and longer portion of each day. How do things change for you when you intentionally cultivate tenderness toward everything you see?

Guess what? You don't have to imagine you are God, because God is in you.

Exercise: Appreciating Life's Uncertainties

One way in which we feed the mind's addiction to suffering is by believing we are fortune-tellers, in complete possession of all the relevant facts concerning our future. We overestimate our ability to predict the outcome of a given situation, and then make ourselves suffer based on this completely imaginary future event. In fact, this is one of the most common ways in which we cause ourselves unnecessary suffering and give up our personal freedom.

A friend of mine suffered greatly when his girlfriend called to tell him that she was leaving in six months to enter a PhD program on the other side of the country. He quickly became fixated on this upcoming change as the single most important issue affecting their long-term prospects as a couple. Although he hadn't been feeling entirely confident about the relationship before she called, he now felt certain that he and his girlfriend had been on a path to living happily ever after *if not for this one terrible change.*

He developed a form of tunnel vision, obsessing over all the wonderful things that would have happened if she hadn't accepted the offer, and all the terrible things that were certain to happen now that she had. It felt as if his whole life were defined by the "problem" of his girlfriend's decision. It was only when his friends dragged him out to play soccer that the fog began to lift. He remembered that he had an entire life outside of this one issue. And he realized that, no matter how many vivid and specific scenarios his mind conjured up, he didn't *actually* know what was going to happen—not tomorrow, and certainly not in six months.

As the fog cleared, he admitted that he and his girlfriend could very well break up for any number of reasons having nothing to do with her departure. On the other hand, six months in the future he might well decide that he felt like moving as well, or they might agree to maintain a long-distance relationship. In short, he began to see that life had infinite possibilities. He didn't have to suffer in response to events that hadn't even happened yet, or that might never happen.

When you are fixated on a single event or situation that you have identified as "the problem," you overestimate your ability to control the outcomes of life and blind yourself to the fact that life will *always* throw you curveballs.

In this exercise, I invite you to stop trying to foresee fixed outcomes and learn to appreciate the infinite possibilites of life.

- Choose a situation in your life that feels like a problem—for example, a change you are resisting.

- Write down the outcome you fear the most as a result of this problem. For example, my friend might write: "My girlfriend is moving across the country. My deepest fear is that this change will cause us to break up."

- Write down all the *other* causes that could lead to the same outcome. My friend might write: "We could also break up because we don't agree about having kids, or because one of us falls in love with someone else, or because we both change."

As difficult as you may find it to write this list, this exercise will help you to see that, even if you manage to "solve" the external problem you've identified, you can never "solve" life's uncertainty except by coming to a place of personal freedom within.

Chapter 6

THE FREEDOM TO DREAM

The modern world places little value on nighttime dreaming. Most parents don't teach their children to pay attention to their dreams. Indeed, many of us have been brought up to believe that our dreams are meaningless, just random brain activity that we're better off ignoring. If we talk about our dreams at all, it's for their entertainment value—"You'll never believe the crazy dream I had last night!" In Western society, most adults would be mortified just to admit that a dream meant something to them, let alone take action based on a dream.

But for thousands of years, in shamanic traditions as well as in all the major religions, dreams were considered to be a perfectly legitimate source of information.

In the Old Testament, Jacob dreams about a ladder reaching from earth to heaven, with angels climbing up and down it. In Islam, the dreams of the prophets are considered to be revelations, as when the prophet Ibrahim dreams of sacrificing his son Isma'il. The ancient Egyptians were obsessive about recording their dreams, and employed oracles whose sole job it was to interpret them. In ancient Greece, dreams were considered a form of medicine, and the sick were encouraged to sleep in special rooms called *enkoimeterion,* where it was thought the gods of healing would send them instructions on how to recover.

In my family's Toltec tradition, dreams are considered to be messages from the Divine. Occasionally, our dreams give us powerful visions, showing us the steps we need to take in our lives. Sometimes they give us messages about our purpose here on earth. Sometimes they put us in touch with our deepest fears, showing us where we still need to heal. As a part of that tradition, I was taught from the time I was very young to pay attention to my dreams.

Ever since my experience with blindness, I've kept a recording device beside my bed. When I wake up from a powerful dream, I hit record and begin narrating the dream in the order it comes to me. Throughout the day, as bits and pieces of the dream come back to me, I record them as well, because I've learned that our dreams don't always make sense all at once. Sometimes when we look back on them a week or a month later, we uncover more and more layers of meaning. This is why I encourage everyone to record their dreams, either in a written dream journal or in voice recordings.

By recording your dreams over a long period of time, you can begin to see patterns. Perhaps a particular animal shows up again and again. Or you may find yourself returning to a certain place in your dreams—a forest, a desert, a city, or even a particular building. You may repeat certain kinds of actions—running away, confronting an aggressor, searching for something, or protecting someone.

Regardless of what you record as the content of your dreams, you can be sure that they are carrying messages for you. It's just a matter of learning to recognize what those messages are.

Message from the Mountain

When I was eleven years old, I had a dream that my father took me to a mountain range called Madre Grande. In the dream, my father stumbled on some rocks and fell. He seemed to be unconscious, or even dead. Terrified, I ran all the way to my mother's house, where I called out: "Mom, Mom, my father is dead! He fell down the mountain!" But just then, my dad came walking up from behind the house, and said: "I'm not dead, I was just playing with you."

A few days later, I asked my father to take me to Madre Grande. He was stunned. He saw it as a sign of power that I had received that dream and asked to be taken to that specific place at such a young age. Shortly thereafter, he took my brother and me to Madre Grande, where we received even more powerful signs from nature. While we were exploring the mountain, I stumbled across a place where four boulders had rolled together, forming a cave-like crevice. My father went into the cave first to make sure it was safe, then called for us to follow him.

As we all sat in the coolness of the cave, my father began to tell us about our family's history and about the principles of Toltec shamanism. He asked if we would like to be initiated into the Toltec lineage. Of course, we both said yes! He then took out some sacred objects and conducted an initiation ceremony. When the ceremony was finished, he stepped out of the cave and stood in the sun, which cast his shadow onto the cave floor. He held his hands over his head so that his shadow formed the shape of a snake, then began to move his body in such a way that the "snake" began to dance.

Suddenly, the entire mountainside was filled with the sound of dozens of rattlesnakes shaking their rattles all at once. My hair stood on end, and my brother and I exchanged a look of fear and awe. "The rattlesnakes have accepted your initiation," my father said. "You are now apprentices to Life."

In the days and weeks following this initiation, I had many more significant dreams, and my path as a shaman became clear.

Dreaming Up Reality

Sometimes our dreams are very clear, and their content leads us to take specific actions in our waking lives. My dream about Madre Grande, for example, led directly to my initiation as a Toltec shaman. But even if your dreams are vague, nonsensical, disorganized, or funny, you can still use them as a vehicle for awakening. Pay attention to the emotions you experience in your dreams. Do you feel fear or panic? Do you feel a sense of confusion, lostness, or curiosity? A sense of wonder, excitement, or pleasure at receiving your heart's desire? These emotions—which can be very intense—are all called forth in response to imaginary events.

But think about this. If your mind is powerful enough to dream up imaginary events when you are asleep and then produce intense emotions in response to them, how much power does it have over your waking life? The same brain that convinces you that you're flying through space, doing battle with monsters, or discovering buried treasure while you're sleeping is also capable of telling you who you are and what you can do in the "real" world. And your brain creates whatever kinds of stories you train it to create. The problem is that most of us don't realize that we're in charge of this powerful dream machine. We let our minds create our reality, complete with its addiction to suffering, instead of learning to create it ourselves.

How many times have you felt intense anxiety within a dream, only to wake up and realize you are perfectly safe? How many times have you woken up from a pleasurable dream, only to be filled with sorrow and yearning to re-enter that blissful state? It is your mind that is creating that sense of safety or danger, that happiness or that misery. When you work with your dreams, you start to recognize that no matter how intense an emotion or situation may be, it will always pass. The next moment will always come. The next dream will always come. It is the quality of your awareness that matters—your ability to meet whatever happens with courage, grace, and sincerity.

In fact, your mind is dreaming all the time—*especially* when you are awake. The events of life are really quite simple. You feel heat and cold, hunger and thirst. You sit, stand, lie down, and walk around. You perform everyday tasks. But it is your dreaming mind that knits these basic events into elaborate dramas in which you are the hero or the victim—in which a person with your name is exalted or disappointed, victorious or betrayed. If you could peer inside somebody else's dream, you would find that *that person* is the hero or the victim, and you are nowhere to be found! How can it be that this character who plays such a huge role in your own dreams—who is subject to being wounded, to winning or losing, to succeeding or failing—is at best a secondary character in others' dreams?

Think about the last time you overheard people having a conversation on a train or in some other public area—the kind in which they vent loudly about some perceived injustice, like being slighted at a fancy restaurant or receiving a less exciting birthday gift than they felt they deserved. To everyone overhearing the conversation, it's painfully clear that the person venting is lost in a dream. Yet, to that person, the problem is the most real and earth-shattering thing going on in the world at that moment.

Or think of the last time a friend of yours fell in love and could talk of nothing except how beautiful, perfect, sexy, and intelligent the person was. It's easy for you to recognize that your friend is infatuated—in other words, caught up in a dream of someone's perfection. But your friend may truly believe that he or she has found the one human being on this planet who possesses no flaws whatsoever.

We're all pretty adept at recognizing when other people are lost in their dreams—whether that takes the form of victimhood, or deep depression, or infatuation, or delusion, or anything else that exaggerates their sense of self-importance and creates a form of tunnel vision. But it takes a lot of practice to recognize when *you* are lost in a dream. And it takes even more to wake up and regain a sense of humor and perspective when you do so.

Dreaming with Awareness

The key is to dream with awareness. Dreaming with awareness means recognizing when you're in an altered state of consciousness. When you drink a mug of strong coffee, you *know* that you're under the influence of caffeine. You may feel alert and energized for an hour or so, your palms may sweat, and you may feel a little jittery. But you know that this is a temporary state, and you don't make the mistake of believing that it is permanent or that your jittery caffeinated self is "who you really are." The problem is that it can be difficult to achieve awareness when you are caught in a dream. And this is true whether those dreams occur when you're asleep or when you're awake.

One good test for whether or not you're caught in a dream is to notice if you're taking things personally. Think of the obnoxious loud talker, convinced that the waiter at the fancy restaurant intentionally brought the wrong wine. Or the infatuated lover, convinced that someone's every action and expression are *all about him or her*. When you are caught in a dream, you tend to exaggerate your own self-importance—especially when it comes to seeking out ways that you have been wounded or wronged, but also when it comes to imagining ways in which you are more special, talented, or enlightened than everyone else.

Another way to determine whether you're caught in a dream is to check if you've started making assumptions. For example, in the dream of depression, it is common to assume negative outcomes for every possible course of action. These assumptions can feel so real and valid that it can be very difficult for you to remember that they are assumptions at all. It can be helpful to ask a friend to point out where you are making assumptions and remind you that you do not, indeed, have a crystal ball that can perfectly predict the future. Not all dreams are bad, of course. For example, if you can keep perspective on a pleasurable state of infatuation, then by all means, enjoy the ride!

Maintaining the awareness that you are dreaming means realizing that the thoughts and feelings you are having right now are temporary, and influenced by the particular flavor of your dream. Whether you are enjoying your dream or suffering inside of it, you know that this dream doesn't reflect who you really are. It's just one possible dream out of many. Who you really are is something much greater than can be contained in any single story or any single dream. Your dreams are just vehicles through which your infinite potential, the nagual, can explore, learn, express itself, and play.

Exercise: Dreaming Intentionally

If you want to bring more intentionality to your nighttime dreams, a great way to start is to simply ask for your dreams to guide you.

- Before going to sleep, make a silent request in your mind: "May my dreams show me what

I need to know." By making this request, you open yourself to receiving wisdom, insights, and messages from your dreams.

- If you don't experience a difference on the first night, make this request with sincerity and humility every night, until you begin to find more meaning in your dreams.

And this practice is not limited to sleeping dreams. When you recognize that you are deep in a waking dream, you can use this simple request to acknowledge that you are dreaming, and to express your openness to learning from the experience. Whether you are in a dream of victimhood or a dream of love, you can always ask it to show you what you need to learn from the experience. "May this dream show me what I need to know." "May this dream teach me what I need to learn."

You can also try keeping a "dream journal" of your waking life, in addition to the journal you keep of your sleeping dreams. A sample entry might read: "Right now, I am having a beautiful dream about being in love. In this dream, my mind is filled with hope, and I have wild thoughts about changing my whole life to be with this person. Being with this person feels like the most important thing I can do, and other things I care about feel like distant memories."

By writing about your waking life as if it were a dream, you can maintain a healthy perspective on this wonderful dream character—yourself! You can experience its many adventures without getting caught up in self-importance or becoming too attached to the story. You can enjoy your dreams and hold them lightly, knowing that they are vehicles for growth.

Exercise: Disarming Nightmares

A friend of mine was troubled by frequent nightmares following a traumatic experience with an ex-boyfriend. She often woke up in the middle of the night with her heart pounding. Sometimes the nightmares were so disturbing that she was afraid to go back to sleep. She began to feel unsafe in her sleep, in the same way that she had once felt unsafe in her waking life.

You can use a variation of the Toltec inventory and recapitulation exercise described in chapter 4 to drain nightmares of their emotional charge, just as you can use it to reclaim the energy that is bound up in challenging memories.

- Write down everything you can remember about your nightmare. What happened? Where did it take place? Who was there? How did you feel? What sounds did you hear? What images did you see?

- You don't have to do this in one sitting. The details of dreams tend to come back in snatches, so give yourself a whole day to recapture whatever you can remember.

- When you feel your dream description is complete, sit or lie in a safe, comfortable place and allow yourself to remember the nightmare in detail.

- As you do so, breathe in all the fear, anxiety, and negative emotion bound up in the nightmare.

- The next time you exhale, imagine yourself expelling only clean, pure energy.

- Pull all the negativity out of the nightmare, cleanse it, and return it to the world as pure energy.

Doing this exercise on a regular basis can help you drain the emotional charge from your nightmares.

You may even find that your nightmares begin to change. For example, although my friend's ex-boyfriend used to show up in her dreams as a powerful and terrifying character, in subsequent dreams, he began to fade—literally. After several weeks of using this practice, he appeared in her dreams as little more than a ghost—translucent, weak, and nearly invisible! By practicing consistently, she took her power back from him and restored it to her own life.

Chapter 7

THE FREEDOM TO CARE

Have you ever seen someone handle a tool, an instrument, or another object in a way that makes you cringe? Perhaps your friend grabs your guitar with greasy hands, turns the tuning pegs roughly, and claws at the strings without paying any attention to the sound. Or your neighbor may buy the best possible power tools, only to leave them out in the rain and otherwise abuse them.

It's hard to watch others treat precious objects in a careless way. "Stop!" you want to say. "Why treat that guitar so badly, when you can treat it well and make it sing? Then you and the guitar will *both* be happier, and so will everyone around you."

As a person who loves playing music, I've always been sensitive to how other people treat instruments. I can't stand to watch someone leave a guitar where it could fall and get damaged, or place a mug of coffee on top of a piano. It just seems wrong to abuse instruments in this way, when they bring us so much pleasure. I've always felt that they take care of us, and we should take care of them as well.

But for most of my life, I didn't realize that the sense of care and respect I bring to my relationship with instruments was utterly missing when it came to my relationship with my own body. I treated my body like the "beater" guitar in a kindergarten classroom—the one we've agreed it's okay to cover in sticky fingerprints, or bang around, or play without skill or awareness.

Instead of recognizing my body for the precious, infinitely complex, and delicate instrument it is, I took it for granted. I treated it as a resource from which I could extract whatever I needed, without putting anything back. Not only did I fail to care for my body, but I took pride in how *little* care I could show it—how late I could stay up drinking, how hard

I could party, how many days or weeks I could go without quality sleep or food.

But that all changed in my early twenties, after I attempted suicide by stabbing myself in the stomach with a steak knife.

Learning to Care

The day I tried to kill myself was the nadir of my disrespect for the beautiful gift of my body. Not only did I fail to care for my body on that day, but I actively tried to annihilate it—like a rock musician smashing his guitar on the stage. Except that, unlike a rock musician, I couldn't just grab another guitar off the rack when I was finished. If I had succeeded at killing my body, that decision would have been final. Although my energy would have persisted in another form, this one precious and specific manifestation of the nagual would have been gone forever, and the pain that would have caused my friends and family would have been impossible to undo.

When I woke up after the surgery that saved my life, my father came to visit me in the hospital. I was embarrassed and immediately began trying to explain myself, telling him all the ways I had been a victim and all the reasons my life had been terrible. He listened intently, and then told me that what I was doing was the equivalent of hitting myself on the head repeatedly while blaming someone else for my misery.

In that moment, I was still angry at myself and at God—angry at life in general. Even though the doctors had saved my life, I wasn't ready to take responsibility for this precious gift. I wasn't ready to be reminded that I was the artist, and was now tasked with creating a new dream. I was still stuck in the old dream—the victim's dream, in which everything that happened to me was somebody else's fault.

The next day, however, something happened that changed my life. I got out of my hospital bed and walked across the room to look at myself in the mirror. I saw the reflection of my face, and a thought came unbidden into my mind: "This person has always been loyal to me. I hurt this person again and again, but look—he's still there. When am I going to start being loyal to *him*?"

As I gazed at my own reflection, I began to feel intense emotions of love, gratitude, and commitment for the body I saw in the mirror. This body had carried me since the day I'd been born. It had done its best to take care of me even when I was abusing myself with drugs and alcohol. It had stuck by me even after I'd stabbed it with a knife. Who could ask for a more loyal, self-sacrificing friend? Yet I hadn't been a friend to my body. I'd used it like a cheap rental car, driving it recklessly and trusting that the insurance would take care of any damage.

In that moment, I saw that my body wasn't *just* mine. It was a piece of the Divine Mother's flesh—a piece of nature. When I hurt myself, I wasn't "only" hurting myself. I was hurting all of creation. Once you have this sort of realization, there is no going back. After you look into your own eyes in a mirror and see divinity gazing back at you, it becomes almost impossible to keep on abusing your body. It's like when people wake up from the dream of drug or alcohol addiction. Once they realize what they've been doing, the high just isn't the same anymore.

Five Hundred Ancestors

In the Toltec tradition, we say that wherever you go, you have five hundred ancestors walking behind you.

Thus, it's important to take care of your body, because it's *their* body too—part of a lineage that has been passed down for countless generations.

Before my grandmother passed away, she called me to her bedside. "Take care of my grandson," she said. By her grandson, of course, she meant me—Jose. After she died, I realized that not only was I a part of her, but she was a part of me as well. When I took care of my own body, I was taking care of the part of my grandmother that still lived in me—and all the ancestors who came before her whose blood was still running through my veins.

Think about it. In order for you to be here today, your distant ancestors all had to survive difficult circumstances, reproduce, and care for their children. Those children then had to survive difficult circumstances, reproduce, and care for *their* children. All those cycles of surviving, reproducing, and caring eventually resulted in your birth—your one chance to experience life in a beautiful, complex, and loyal body, here on planet earth.

Buddhists have a wonderful story about how lucky we are to experience human birth. The tale describes a vast beach on which rests a huge pile of sand, taller than the eye can see. Every thousand years, a bird flies over this beach and picks up a single grain of sand in its beak. Buddhists believe that getting to experience life in a human body is just as rare a gift as being the single grain of sand the bird picks up on its once-every-thousand-year journey over the beach. The other grains of sand become plants, animals, and other forms of life—beautiful, but unable to experience love the way humans do.

Whether or not you believe in reincarnation, this story contains an important message. Being a human on this planet is a very special experience, so we shouldn't take our bodies for granted. In fact, we should do everything in our power to care for them, because they allow us to carry out our calling and create the artwork of our lives. When we care for our bodies, we send ourselves a message of love and respect that penetrates to the deepest level. The day that you look at yourself in a mirror and tell your body that you are not going to hurt it anymore—that you are going to be loyal to it—that's the day your entire relationship to life starts to change.

Over the years since I had my own realization, I've lost over one hundred pounds. I've changed my eating habits and I no longer ingest any drugs or alcohol. Some people who knew me warned me that I'd never be able to accomplish this. They were attached to the old image they had of me—the overweight Jose, the Jose who didn't care about his health. Even when they wanted the best for me, they were still startled to see me shapeshift in this way. It's human nature to resist change, even the positive change we see in others. For me, I had to come to a point where my body wasn't working before I knew it was time to unlearn my old ways.

Now, I no longer crave my past indulgences, because I prefer to be healthy. I love the way my body feels when I take care of it. I feel good knowing that my ancestors are happy inside of this healthy body. The macho culture in which I grew up, the culture that teaches people identified as male at birth to treat their bodies like monster trucks, to be smashed and destroyed in any random way—I don't have to live according to that dream anymore. I have the freedom to care for myself, for this piece of the Divine that has been entrusted to me.

The Ritual of Caring

Caring for your body can take the form of a ritual. You probably already carry out several of these rituals throughout the day without even being aware of it. For example, when you wake up in the morning, you take a shower, brush your teeth, drink your tea or coffee, and eat your breakfast. These may not seem like religious acts, but they are rituals because they are about taking care of your body and preparing yourself to bring your best effort to the day. The moment you do anything with love and respect, that act becomes a ritual act.

In *The Four Agreements*, my father writes about his love of ritual, especially as it pertains to taking care of his body:

> Taking a shower is a ritual for me, and with that action I tell my body how much I love it. I feel and enjoy the water on my body. I do my best to fulfill the needs of my body. I do my best to give to my body and to receive what my body gives to me.

Think of the tender way you'd care for a baby, a lover, a sick friend, or an elderly grandparent. Can you invoke that same spirit of tenderness when you care for your own body? When you give a baby a bath or give your lover a massage, there is often a sense of ritual to the action. You may put some lavender oil in the baby's bathwater or light candles for your lover. You take your time and go slowly, instead of rushing through the task. You savor the act of bringing comfort and pleasure to this other being.

But here's the thing—you are your own baby. You are your own lover. You are your own friend. You are your own elder.

This body is the love of your life, and it is always speaking to you. Feel the ways in which your body is communicating with you; learn to listen. Once you begin to feel that life force, you become aware of all the acts you do that either support your body or go against it. Many of us have been domesticated since childhood to ignore our physical needs, even our physical pain. But as we walk the path to personal freedom, we realize the importance of unlearning these habits.

Even if you can't avoid hurting your body sometimes, by accident or overuse, you can do your best to protect it from injury, keep it well-nourished and well-rested, and do the things that bring it joy.

Sometimes it can be helpful to think about your body in the third person. "Jose is going to need a nap." "Jose needs to get some exercise this afternoon." If you've been domesticated to believe that it's selfish to care for your own body but that it's okay to care for somebody else's, try thinking about yourself in the third person. This can help you learn to see yourself as a person who is deserving of care. After all, you're not making tea for yourself—you're making tea for a very special person, a person who happens to have the same name you do!

When you do your best to take care of your body, it becomes lighter and happier. You experience more love, because you're giving more love. You send yourself a deep message that you are safe, respected, and adored. And this prepares you to be a messenger of love for the whole world.

Exercise: Experiencing Your Body as Nature

The mind's addiction to suffering deepens whenever we latch on to a specific identity and forget that we are a part of nature, just as much as the rocks and trees. Rocks and trees don't suffer, because they never question the validity of their own existence. They can express themselves completely, in all kinds of different forms, never resisting the forces of change. We humans, on the other hand, tend to collect ideas about who we are, in the same way that we collect burrs on our pant legs when we walk through tall grass. We forget that we can brush all those burrs away and still be whole, complete, and perfect, just like any other element of nature.

In this exercise, I invite you to experience your body in a pure form, independent of any ideas about who you are.

- Find a comfortable place to sit where you won't be disturbed for at least twenty minutes. This can be at a table or in a chair. You don't have to sit in a traditional posture of meditation.

- Place one hand where you can see it, either by laying it on the table in front of you, placing it in your lap, or holding it in front of your face if that's comfortable for you.

- For the next ten minutes, simply gaze at your hand. Really pay attention to it, as if it's a new and fascinating object you have never seen before. If you want to move your hand, you can curl and uncurl your fingers, or move it closer to and then farther away from your eyes. Try to look at your hand with the same appreciation you would give to a beautiful flower you stumbled upon in the forest, or a new kind of seashell you found on the beach.

- After doing this for a few minutes, allow yourself to feel a sense of awe and tenderness toward this intricate, ingeniously designed piece of artwork—your own hand. Notice its beauty in a way you never did before. Feel gratitude for all the ways it has been useful to you over the course of your life.

- Tilt your head and gaze down at your body as a whole. For ten minutes, allow yourself to experience your whole body as a part of nature. Observe it the same way you would observe a wild animal or a rippling

waterfall. Allow yourself to see your own
body as something mysterious, divine, and
in a constant process of change.

This exercise can help you break free of old patterns of domestication and nourish the roots of personal freedom. Knowing that you are a part of nature, you can no longer be defined by any particular identity or mask. Underneath all the identities you've inhabited and all the masks you've worn, your body has always been there—pure, ever changing, and impossible to confine in a single story.

Exercise: Cultivating Joy

Although the addiction to suffering arises in our minds, we sometimes perpetuate it in our relationship with our bodies as well. Just as we can seek out negative mental states simply because they are familiar, many of us do the same thing with physical states. For example, I doubt that many people actually *enjoy* the feeling of being hungover, or eating too much food, or not getting adequate rest. Yet many of us find a strange kind of comfort in these unpleasant states because they are familiar.

But once you begin to establish a state of joy and pleasure in your body, your attraction to these unpleasant states quickly fades and you begin to wonder why you ever punished yourself in that way.

In this exercise, I invite you to cultivate joy in your physical being.

- Find a place where you will not be disturbed. This can be a room indoors or a quiet place in nature. The key is to be there by yourself.

- Put on some music you love, whether on speakers or on headphones.

- For the next five to ten minutes, dance to the music.

For some, this may come quite easily. For others, it may bring up deep feelings of shame, sorrow, and resistance. You may find yourself standing stiffly, unwilling to move your body. You may even feel intensely anxious. For those who were domesticated to use their bodies only for work or other "serious" purposes, it can be frightening and unfamiliar to use them for play.

Please believe me that, no matter who you are or how long it has been since you've experienced your body as a source of pleasure, it is your basic human right to dance. My sincere wish is that you will stick with this exercise until you unlock the joy that is yours to claim.

You can also cultivate joy in your body by assuming good posture, grooming and adorning yourself with care, exercising or playing sports, and engaging in physical labor that raises your spirits and gets you out of your head.

Moving our bodies produces endorphins in the brain that help us feel better—or, as the shamans in my family would say, help us break the mind's addiction to suffering. The more we cultivate joy as a baseline, the less soil we provide in which the addiction to suffering can take root. Respecting the body-mind connection is key.

Chapter 8

THE FREEDOM TO ACCEPT

A dear friend of mine married his college sweetheart and, together, they were raising a beautiful daughter. As they approached their thirteenth anniversary, his wife sat him down at the kitchen table and said: "I'm sorry. I know this will hurt you, but I am not in love with you anymore. I am in love with someone else." He was shocked. He begged and pleaded for her to reconsider. He talked about their daughter, the vows they had made, and how he believed they would be together forever. He offered to attend couples counseling, make internal changes, and do anything she wanted, but it was all to no avail. She was finished with the relationship in its current form.

My friend continued to fight his impending separation with all his might, until one day he ran into an old friend—an old cowboy—who cordially inquired about his family. Although he had hidden the situation from everyone he knew in the hope that it would change, he blurted out the entire story, explaining everything in detail, including all he had done to try to "fix" the situation. The man listened intently and then said: "Well, son, it looks like the horse is going the other way."

Like being struck on the shoulders with a Zen priest's *keisaku*, the cowboy's words caused my friend to wake up. He realized that he was putting all his energy into denial, instead of engaging with his life as it really was. He was clinging to an old dream even as this dream shriveled up before his eyes. He was also fueling his mind's addiction to suffering, preferring to torment himself with the "problem" of his wife's decision rather than accepting this change as a valid element in the artwork of his life.

Indeed, my friend hadn't realized that *accepting* this change was even an option. He'd been domesticated to believe that a man should fight for his marriage at all costs. This domestication limited his personal freedom, blinding him to the infinite possibilities that still remained to him in life, and causing him to forget the nagual within. In other words, he didn't realize he had the *freedom* to accept.

In the days and weeks following his encounter with the old cowboy, my friend began to move from denial to acceptance. Although he had a lot of grieving to do, he simultaneously became aware of all the new possibilities that were opening to him now that his life was no longer defined by the old dream. For example, he had always wanted to start playing the guitar again, but his wife preferred to watch movies in the evening. He wanted to adopt a cat, something his wife had always been firmly against. In the wake of their separation, he finally got to pursue both these dreams—and that was only the beginning of what proved to be a wonderful new life. Some years later, he remarried and had two more children, blessings that would never have come if he had not moved on from his old dream.

The power of acceptance doesn't get much attention in the modern world, because it is often confused with giving up. We don't want to be quitters, and it can be hard to tell when we've crossed the line between simply doing our best and entering into the realm of denial. In cases like this, it helps to have a wise observer provide some outside perspective. Often, this is a trusted friend who can help you see your situation more clearly. But sometimes you simply arrive at that clarity on your own.

In my own case, I experienced sexual abuse as a young teenager. Where I grew up in Tijuana, Mexico, the culture of *machismo* made it extremely difficult to admit to myself or anyone else that I had been victimized. I pushed this knowledge down for many years, hiding it in a dark corner of my mind. My inability to accept what had happened meant that I couldn't heal from it, and I couldn't help others heal or speak out against the *machismo* culture that is so destructive to both men *and* women.

When I finally found the courage to face the truth of what had happened to me and tell someone about it, mountains of emotional and physical stress dropped away practically overnight. I hadn't realized that by suppressing this truth, I was forcing it to manifest as illness in my body in the form of overeating, nightmares, and other physical symptoms. Acceptance freed my body from the terrible burden of carrying this secret around, and restored a torrent of trapped energy that I could now put into music, friendship, and the ongoing work of being the artist of my life.

Medicine Bags

In my family's shamanic tradition, we sometimes work with medicine bags. These are small pouches filled with objects that are significant to you—beautiful stones, a feather, a crystal, a coin. In some cases, these objects represent challenges you're addressing, like developing courage, recovering from an illness, or pursuing some goal. As your inner work evolves, the contents of your medicine bag may change. You may take out an object that represents an issue that you feel has been resolved, or you may put in something new. I've owned several medicine bags in my life, including one given to me by my father, one given to me by my grandmother, and another that is filled with small objects I've collected from power places around the world.

While physical medicine bags are very effective as tangible reminders of your spiritual path, the most important medicine bag of all is your heart. No matter where you go, your heart acts like an internal medicine bag, holding your relationships, your intentions, and the wounds from which you are healing. At any given moment, you are working with a certain set of items in this internal medicine bag, all of which are there to teach you something and help you grow. Sometimes an item may represent a quality that you will pursue throughout your life. For example, you may spend your whole life working on unconditional love. In other cases, an item may represent something that is causing you pain, and it takes wisdom to recognize when you should let these items go. That's where the power of acceptance comes into play.

From Denial to Acceptance

When we are feeling pain from a source we can't acknowledge—and this includes everything from an abusive relationship, to a dark secret, or even working at a job long after it's time to move on—our energy gets trapped in the form of denial, the way water can freeze into ice. Think of a frozen pipe that can no longer deliver drinking water to the occupants of a house. The water is still there, but it's not useful if it doesn't flow.

People who have been in denial for a long time are often amazed at how much their lives improve when they move into acceptance. New opportunities open up; stagnant relationships begin to evolve; health conditions ameliorate. Once you get past the emotional pain associated with the truth you've been denying, the world begins to sparkle with possibility. Denial is fuel for the mind's addiction to suffering, and acceptance is the first step toward being able to dance with the flow of life. When you move past denial, you can remove old items from your medicine bag and find new things to love and enjoy. When you move into acceptance, you open yourself to the rich possibilities of life.

When we start to accept our own truths, we naturally learn how to accept the truths of others, instead of using their actions and words to cause ourselves pain. A few years ago, a partner of mine made the decision to separate from me. Before I'd discovered the freedom to accept, I would have felt very upset about her decision. I would have used it as an opportunity to hurt myself. "She doesn't love me; she's abandoning me." "I will never have enduring love in my life." Perhaps, like my friend, I would have tried to convince her to stay, or told her all the reasons her decision was bad or wrong. I would have denied her truth and tried to replace it with my own.

But by viewing our relationship as one beautiful and temporary item in my medicine bag, I was able to accept her feelings instead of trying in vain to change them. She needed the space to blossom as her own person, to create her own art. If I tried to deny this, I would be hurting her *and* myself, while failing to learn the lessons this item in my medicine bag was trying to teach me. Thanks to the power of acceptance, I kept loving my partner and wanting the best for her, even as she made a decision that was not what I would have chosen.

A couple of years after this experience, my father had a serious heart attack and everyone believed that he was going to die. When I went to visit him in the hospital, I came into the room crying and said: "Please don't die, Father, please don't die." He gave me a stern look and said: "Jose, is this how you celebrate the death of your father? Go outside and collect yourself. And when you're ready, come back, because I need to talk to you before I go."

My father correctly perceived that I was in a state of denial—a frightened, contracted state in which he wouldn't be able to communicate with me heart-to-heart. I left the room and collected myself. "Jose," I said to myself, "your father may die today, and he will definitely die *someday*." Even though I felt a stab of emotional pain as I contemplated these truths, I felt myself coming out of my contracted state and returning to my higher self.

When I returned to the room, I said: "Father, thank you so much. I see that I almost wasted what might be the last few moments of your life mired in self-pity and denial, right when I needed to be present with you." He thanked me for having the wisdom to recognize what had happened, and we enjoyed an intimate conversation together. As it happened, my father did *not* die on that day, but the lesson I learned has stayed with me ever since.

Lessons from the River

One of the stories that has been passed down in my family for generations is the story of the Riverman. It tells of a young man who falls in love with a beautiful woman at the time of the second Mayan empire. One day, he comes home to discover that his beloved has been offered as a human sacrifice. She has already been slain, and he is too late to save her. Nearly mad with grief and guilt over not having protected her, he retreats to the jungle, where he refuses to eat or sleep. After several days of sitting alone and crying, he walks to the edge of a rushing river and jumps in, hoping to drown himself.

As he sinks below the churning water, he sees the face of his beloved. He calls out to her in joy: "My love! I've found you! I promise I'll never let you out of my sight again."

But the spirit of his beloved replies: "You cannot stay with me, and if you carry out your intention of drowning in this river, you will never see me again. If you want to join me where I am, you must stop living in the pain of the past."

The young man awakes to find himself on the riverbank, soaking wet and gasping for air. He realizes that what his beloved said is true. He cannot join her in the heaven of love as long as he is trapped in the hell of denial, refusing to accept that she is gone. In that moment, his heart opens and he forgives the fanatical people who sacrificed his beloved to their god of war. He feels the beauty of the jungle and the peace of the river, and knows that she is with him in spirit. He resolves to end his own suffering, and to go forward and live as she would have wanted him to live.

So many times, we are just like this young man. We are always looking for what the river swept away—a lost love, a failed endeavor, an old identity—instead of accepting the reality of the loss and focusing on what the river may bring next. We forget that no matter how great and tragic our loss, we retain the power to create and the power to choose. Although the river may sweep away everything we hold dear on the external plane, it can never take away the fundamental power we have to determine the artwork of our own lives.

A friend of mine was devastated after she lost her ability to walk following a car accident. She had been an avid hiker and rock climber, and the grief and despair she felt as a result of her loss nearly killed her. She truly felt that her life was over, and she saw no point in going on. But with encouragement from friends, she began to realize that her life *wasn't* over. The river was still carrying new opportunities toward her every single day. She got a pair of binoculars and started watching birds, and ended up getting heavily involved with her local bird-watching group. She also became involved in a movement to make hiking trails more accessible to people in wheelchairs, and made some of her closest friends because of that work. Like the Riverman, she chose to live in the heaven of the present moment, instead of the hell of denial and regrets.

Embracing the Journey

One of my favorite things to do while traveling is to wander around a foreign city without looking at a map. I just decide upon some destination—a cathedral, a museum, a park—and then try to make my way there by instinct. I love the feeling of getting slightly or even *very* lost, wandering in circles, ending up in places I never expected to be, and even stumbling upon my original destination after having completely given up hope of finding it.

These wanderings have helped me discover that when you have inner peace, it really doesn't matter where you're going. Some of my most beautiful travel experiences have taken place in strange little alleys and ramshackle gardens, not in the grand destinations on my to-do list. In fact, the opposite has proven to be true. Some of my most *stressful* travel experiences happened when I went exactly where I planned to go and did exactly what I'd planned to do! What matters is the quality of our energy as we move through the world, not the specific place we end up.

Think of the last time you ended up in a completely different place from where you thought you wanted to be. Perhaps you set out intending to be single for a while, but then you met the love of your life. Or you visited a beautiful place, planning to stay for only a week, but then you decided to move there. Or you stopped by an animal shelter to bring coffee to a friend and left with two adopted puppies who filled your whole life with joy. This is the magic of embracing life as a journey. It's not about arriving at the destination; it's about opening yourself to whatever happens along the way. And this requires the ability to accept each moment as it comes.

The Challenges of Acceptance

One of the most challenging and humbling aspects of acceptance is learning that we cannot control the actions, feelings, or opinions of others, no matter how badly we wish to do so. For example, we may wish to "save" our children from bad decisions, or "correct" somebody's version of events that we believe is far less accurate than our own. But even when we feel that our intentions for others are noble, as Toltecs we remember that we are each the artists of our own lives; we are *not* the artists of other peoples' lives. We know that we don't get to write anyone else's story. On the contrary, we choose to respect that the people around us will *always* have the power to choose for themselves, to create their own art.

Accepting this truth takes a great deal of humility. Perhaps a family member insists on seeing you in a certain way long after you've changed. Or a friend misunderstands your spiritual path, no matter how much care you put into explaining it. You may see that someone you love is making choices that will likely cause them great heartache and suffering, no matter what warnings they have received. For many of us, love is deeply tied up with control. We express our love by trying to force others to act in ways that align with our own convictions, and it can be terribly difficult to accept that they have the right to make harmful choices.

A woman I know suffered greatly when her husband began abusing pills to deal with his stress at work. Like many partners of addicts, she tried to "help" him by hiding his stash or arguing with him over the amount he was consuming each day. As the situation worsened, she was forced to accept that she could not "save" him from what proved to be a disastrous breakdown. She could only control her own actions and decisions, and take steps to protect herself from harm.

Another challenging facet of acceptance is learning to accept help from others. Many of us are domesticated from childhood to be self-reliant. We don't want to seem weak or needy, so we avoid asking for help. We fear the vulnerability of letting others know we need them, instead of cherishing the opportunity to strengthen our social bonds. Yet opportunities to give and receive help constitute some of the most meaningful experiences of our lives.

Think of a time when you helped a friend or loved one—picking a family member up in the middle of a snowstorm, or visiting a friend in the hospital every day, or helping to put a new roof on a neighbor's house. For many of us, these acts of love and sacrifice are the most precious memories we possess. Far from resenting or regretting someone's need for help, we benefited from the opportunity to share our gifts.

The next time you need help, consider the fact that the person helping *you* is probably enjoying some of these same emotional and spiritual benefits. When you feel free to accept help from others, you honor the nagual and contribute something positive to the world. You also free others to accept help from you.

Exercise: Learning to Trust

Acceptance often means taking a leap from the safe and familiar into the unknown—and this requires a great deal of trust. There are many times when we need to accept things that we didn't anticipate and wouldn't necessarily have chosen. Practicing acceptance means greeting your whole life with unconditional love and moving forward with trust.

One way to build this trust is to recognize that the *fact* of acceptance is separate from your story about the condition or situation being accepted. This is just like learning to differentiate between emotions and reactions. Remember the lesson that my friend learned from the old cowboy. He feared that if he accepted the end of his marriage, he would be doomed to a lifetime of loneliness. In other words, he created a *story* about what his life would be like if he accepted this turn of events. And for a long time, this story kept him from letting go of the old dream. But when he let go of the story and stuck to the facts—"My marriage has ended"—he regained his personal freedom and eliminated unnecessary suffering around this turn of events.

Many of our stories take the form of if/then statements that feed the mind's addiction to suffering. "If I accept that my relationship has ended, I'll be lonely forever." "If I let my neighbor help me, he'll know how incompetent I am." This exercise helps you use the power of language to diffuse this tendency.

- In your journal, write down something in your life that you are having trouble accepting.

- Write down your assumptions about how this issue will play out. In other words, make a prediction about it.

- Rephrase this prediction as a question. "What would happen if my relationship ended?" "What would it be like if I asked my neighbor for help?"

- Feel into some possible answers to these questions while remaining open to the idea that whatever life brings, it will be for your ultimate good.

By transforming your assumptions into questions, you open yourself to being surprised by life. You also give other people the opportunity to surprise you—by being far more accepting, supportive, and skillful than you expected.

When you refrain from making assumptions, you open up space in which *anything* can happen—including many beautiful things you could never have predicted. You can accept the truth of your life, knowing that this vulnerability will only bring you greater safety, connection, and joy.

Exercise: The Five Remembrances

Buddhists have a beautiful practice called the Five Remembrances that encourages acceptance of the inevitable changes of life. The practice consists of repeating the following phrases every day:

> I am of the nature to grow old; there is no escaping old age.

> I am of the nature to experience injury and sickness; there is no escaping ill health.

> I am of the nature to die; there is no escaping death.

> I am of the nature to be separated from all that is dear to me and everyone I love.

> My only true belongings are my actions.

When you meditate on these phrases, you remind yourself that aging, sickness, death, and loss are not aberrations. They are, in fact, fundamental aspects of the human experience, just as they are part of the experience of all living beings. When you accept this truth at a deep level, you experience less suffering when these events occur.

Note that the Buddhist phrasing includes the words "of the nature." When you work with this practice, this reminds you that old age, disease, and death link you to nature. Indeed, the planet wouldn't function without them!

Now I invite you to adapt this Buddhist practice to include the specific things that you struggle to accept about yourself or about life in general, then add the phrase "and that's okay" to each of these statements.

I am of the nature to grow old . . . and that's okay.

I am of the nature to experience injury and sickness . . . and that's okay.

I am of the nature to die . . . and that's okay.

I am of the nature to be separated from all that is dear to me and everyone I love . . . and that's okay.

My only true belongings are my actions . . .
and that's okay.

Repeat these phrases to yourself every day, and remember that it's all okay.

This practice helps you deepen your acceptance of life and find more joy within life's constraints. You can also deepen your empathy for others who are likewise subject to these universal experiences of loss, discomfort, and change.

Chapter 9

THE FREEDOM TO FORGIVE

Most stories about forgiveness focus on the benefits of forgiving others. But consider this Buddhist tale, which sees forgiveness from a different perspective.

One day, the Buddha was sitting with his disciples when an angry man came right up to him and spat in his face. Buddha's disciples were horrified by this behavior, but the Buddha himself just cocked his head and asked the man: "What else?"

The next day, the same man came back. But this time, instead of spitting in the Buddha's face, he bowed down and humbly begged his forgiveness.

"How can I forgive you?" the Buddha asked. "The man who spat on me yesterday isn't here today. And the person who got spat on isn't here either. Nobody has been insulted, and there is nobody to forgive."

This story shows that when you are living in complete awareness, there is no need to forgive others, because you cannot be harmed in the first place. There is no constant and identifiable "self" to be insulted or offended, and no constant and identifiable "other" who can do the offending. The Buddha knows that the angry man isn't spitting on *him*. He's spitting on an idea which may or may not have anything to do with the real Buddha. In other words, the Buddha refuses to take it personally.

At the same time, the Buddha recognizes that the man's anger is a temporary state—a passing reflection in the mirror. He knows there is nothing to gain from rubbing the man's face in his bad behavior. Clearly he already regrets his actions, because he has come back to ask forgiveness. But even more important, the Buddha knows that the man is living inside his own dream, and nothing can be said or done to change that. What happened is in the past; now the only way to go is forward.

How many times have you clung to your anger against someone, only to run into that person months or years later and realize that the person at whom you've been angry isn't even there anymore? How many times have you insisted on being wounded by someone else's mistake, creating a "self" for the sole purpose of being harmed or offended?

When you forgive others, you not only free up the energy that was going into hating or fearing them, but you also come into your true nature, which is limitless, unbounded, and in some ways invincible. You realize that although other people's actions may hurt you in the moment, they can only cause you lasting harm to the degree that you take them personally.

Forgiving Yourself

The greatest act of forgiveness in my own life was forgiving myself for all the ways in which I'd gone against myself—through my words, through my actions, and through my lack of care for my own body and mind. It was hard to come to terms with the fact that the worst abuser in my life was me, Jose. It wasn't some outside bully—it was me!

This realization is hardly unique to me. I hear it from my apprentices all the time. For example, one apprentice came to me several times over the years complaining that her husband didn't listen: "No matter how much care and skill I put into telling him what I need and what's not working for me, he never changes! It's as if he doesn't hear a single word I say." Finally, she made the decision to leave the relationship. A few months later, she came to me and said: "I realized that the whole time I was complaining about my husband not listening to me, I wasn't listening to *myself.* All along, a voice inside was telling me to leave and I wouldn't listen. The person who really let me down was *me!*"

For a while, this woman struggled with guilt and regret about her failure to listen to her own instincts. But after another couple of months, she came to me again. "Jose," she said, "I've forgiven myself for failing to listen and taking so long to leave. At the time, I truly believed that it was better to override my own instincts and try to work things out. I was doing my best according to my level of awareness at that time, and I want to honor myself for doing my best."

If you have a hard time forgiving yourself for past mistakes, it can be helpful to consider the ways in which you were doing your best based on the awareness you had at that time. You may have yelled at your children because you truly believed it would keep them safe. Or perhaps you chose to abuse your mind and body in a stressful job because you truly believed that financial security was the key to life. But if you were doing your best in these circumstances, there is no reason to punish yourself. Simply acknowledge that, given the growth in your awareness, you would no longer make the same choices. Then forgive yourself.

It can be difficult for some to realize the extent to which they abuse themselves, because this abuse can often take the form of very subtle mental processes rather than dramatic external behaviors. For example, you may have a story buried deep inside that you are unworthy because of a past choice or event. Based on this story, you may think that you should not have love, success, friendship, or good health. You may be so habituated to the presence of this story that you don't even realize it's there—like some familiar piece of furniture you never think to inspect closely. Until your awareness is very sharp, you may only have fleeting glimpses of clarity in which the story comes into focus.

A friend of mine grew up feeling that she was a burden on her distracted parents, and this feeling quietly solidified into a belief that she was a burden on *everyone*, including those closest to her. She avoided reaching out for any kind of connection, because she assumed that this constituted an outrageous "demand" with a high likelihood of being rejected. Meanwhile, she observed that other people she knew were constantly reaching out to one another—chatting, asking for help, exchanging jokes, giving and receiving favors.

For a while, she simply adapted this observation to fit her existing story. *Other* people weren't burdensome, she concluded, but *she* was. Fortunately, it wasn't long before the absurdity of this belief became impossible to ignore. She realized that this subtle conviction had been running her life for years, cutting her off from the connection she needed. She grieved all the ways she'd passed up opportunities for love and friendship over her lifetime and vowed to let herself bring these blessings into her life going forward.

The best thing to do when you're feeling intense regret about a choice you made is to remember that the person who made that mistake in the past is not here anymore. The person who is here *today* has woken up and is not going to make the same mistakes or make them with the same frequency.

Although it is good to take responsibility for your actions, and to look with wise remorse on the mistakes you've made, shaming or punishing yourself isn't helpful. It is simply a manifestation of the mind's addiction to suffering. Shame and guilt for past actions are only useful in that they show you the behaviors you do not wish to repeat. When you look at your actions with wise remorse, you can grow and change in ways that benefit those you have hurt.

Forgiving Others

Once we forgive ourselves, it becomes easier to forgive others. Just as we were caught under the spell of unhealthy agreements when we abused ourselves, the people who hurt or abused us were likewise operating from unhealthy agreements when they carried out their harmful acts. This doesn't mean that their actions were okay. But it can help us to understand how they were able to make such grave mistakes. Just like us, they were domesticated in a certain way and subject to making unconscious agreements they never had the opportunity to question.

A friend of mine was raised in a household in which he and his siblings were often hit by their parents in anger. After much reflection, he realized that both of his parents had a deep fear of being humiliated. They were afraid their children would misbehave and embarrass them in public, and they had an unconscious agreement that they would do whatever it took to prevent this from happening, even if it meant controlling their children through fear and violence. He also realized that both of his parents had been domesticated to believe that the job of a parent was to control the child, and the job of the child was to submit to the parent's control.

My friend realized he was very lucky compared to his parents. He had the gift of awareness, which allowed him to see these patterns for what they were. This awareness ensured that he would never do the same thing to his own children. His parents, on the other hand, had never had the opportunity to develop their own awareness. They had spent most of their lives in a state of blindness, hurting themselves and others without knowing a better way.

If you're struggling to forgive someone who has hurt you, start by being grateful for your own awareness. Awareness is a precious gift. We don't all receive equal opportunities to cultivate it. If you're lucky enough to have it, you will eventually begin to feel pity and even tenderness toward those who don't. Imagine how painful it must be to live life without awareness—hurting yourself and others, your mind filled with emotional poison you don't know how to control. As the Buddha said: "To understand everything is to forgive everything." Once you understand the pain and delusion in which your abusers are living, it becomes much easier to forgive them.

Forgiving Past Trauma

A dear friend of mine is a Buddhist monk from Cambodia who came to the United States as a teenager after surviving the Khmer Rouge regime of the late 1970s, under which it is estimated that over a million people were killed. Before escaping to the United States, he watched his entire immediate family die at the hands of Khmer soldiers.

When I asked him how he dealt with such an unspeakable trauma, he replied: "Well, I try not to think about it."

He went on to explain that although he didn't spend his time *thinking* about these horrifying events, he was fully willing to feel the intense sadness and grief they caused when they came up. But once the feelings had arisen and passed, he didn't subject himself to more suffering by continuing to ruminate on the tragedy. In this way, he allowed himself to feel when he needed to, without feeding his mind's addiction to suffering.

His words impacted me greatly, because I realized that even when such unspeakable tragedies occur, there comes a point when we transition from genuine grieving and processing to mere ruminating and rehashing—in other words, we feed the mind's addiction to suffering. When it comes to forgiveness, it's helpful to do as my monk friend did and allow yourself to feel the emotions associated with the harm without getting sucked into *thinking* about all the ways a person or group has done you wrong. This allows you to forgive cleanly and completely, instead of circling around the wound again and again.

I also want to be clear that forgiving others does not mean removing all boundaries with them. For example, you may forgive those who abused you in some way while still maintaining strict boundaries around your interactions (or non-interactions) with them. Although forgiveness sometimes involves letting others know you have forgiven them, it can also be a completely internal, private process. Indeed, the person you forgive doesn't even need to know that you did it.

When you become aware, you feel compassion for those in your life who are unaware. You begin to see the ways in which their actions sprang from ignorance, domestication, the addiction to suffering, and harmful agreements. You stop hurting yourself with shame and anger, and enter an expansive space in which forgiveness is possible—for yourself, your family, your partner, and even people you've never met.

The Empty Boat

One beautiful Zen story tells of a man who is out fishing on the ocean when another fishing boat knocks into his own.

"Hey," the fisherman says, shaking his fist. "Watch where you're going!"

The other boat hits his again, chipping the paint.

"I'm warning you, buddy," says the fisherman, getting angry.

The other boat collides with his boat again, splintering off a piece of the hull.

"That's it!" he says, truly enraged now. "I'm gonna kick your ass!"

The fisherman leans over the side of his boat to see who this scoundrel is—only to realize that the other boat is empty. In fact, it is weathered and old, and looks as if it's been floating around for months, completely abandoned. There is no one to blame for the damage to his boat, and nobody to fight. The event was completely random!

Remember the image of the empty boat whenever you feel tempted to take things personally. In our imaginations, the events of our lives seem to be "all about us." But are they?

A friend of mine lost her house in a wildfire, while several of her neighbors' houses survived. Although she grieved the loss of her home, the real suffering came from tormenting herself with the question: "Why me?" Had she done something wrong to provoke this terrible event? Did she have bad karma? Was it cosmic punishment for being greedy, or selfish, or having some other character flaw? Why did her house burn down, yet her neighbors' houses were left standing? The more personal she made her loss, the more she suffered.

That's often how our minds work. When negative situations arise, we create a story of wrongdoing and look for someone or something to blame. In the case of my friend, it was only when she began to see the loss of her house as an empty boat that her suffering began to subside.

You can learn not to take things personally by changing how you think and speak. Instead of saying "My parents abused me," you can say "I know what it's like to grow up in a violent household." Instead of saying "My house burned down," you can say "I know what it's like to lose your home in a fire." When you think and speak in this way, you remember that these experiences are just empty boats floating around in the ocean of life. They can happen to anyone and you can forgive them, knowing they're not about you. Furthermore, these events, while tragic and not something you would have chosen, often lead to gifts that you couldn't have received in any other way. This is an example of the great tapestry of life, where tragedy is interwoven with blessings in ways that we cannot always predict.

Exercise: Visualizing Forgiveness

If there are people you want to forgive but no longer have access to, or simply don't want to interact with in real life, you can still carry out a ritual of forgiveness.

- Visualize those who hurt you. If there are specific incidents associated with this pain, recall them to your mind.

- Imagine meeting the highest selves of these people in the ethereal realm.

- If it feels safe, imagine that they have gained the necessary awareness and now wish to apologize for hurting you. What would they say to you if they were truly speaking from their highest selves? What would you say to them, if you could be sure their highest selves would hear it?

- ◆ Write an imaginary letter to yourself from the highest selves of those who harmed you. You can also write a response or dialog with them.

- ◆ Once you've completed this, place a hand over your heart and say: "I forgive you for what happened. May you develop the awareness to understand the harm that you've done and stop causing harm in the future. May you develop the awareness to detach from your old agreements and create a better dream."

Remember that you're perfectly safe as you do this, and that the forgiveness you offer here is for you, so that you can create peace in your own dream.

Exercise: Cultivating Compassion

When my friend's adult son committed suicide, he tormented himself with the thought that there was something he could have done to prevent it. No matter how many times his friends, his therapist, and his spiritual teachers told him that the tragedy wasn't his fault, he couldn't forgive himself for "allowing" it to happen.

Two months after his son's death, he attended a support group for parents who had lost children to suicide. As the participants went around the circle sharing their stories, he heard other parents blaming themselves for their children's deaths, just as he'd been blaming himself. As he listened, he felt tremendous empathy for them, because it was obvious to him that these deaths were not their fault. He could see that they felt genuine remorse for the ways in which they felt they'd let their children down, and he understood that they were now endlessly tormenting themselves for those completely normal mistakes.

After the meeting, my friend went up to a participant whose story had moved him deeply, gave him a big hug, and said sincerely: "Brother, it wasn't your fault." The man burst into tears and hugged him back.

That night, my friend went home and had a deep, healing cry. Just as he had absolved the other parent at the meeting, he finally felt able to absolve himself. "It wasn't your fault," he said out loud as he cried. He forgave himself for the ways he had let his son down, knowing that it would have been impossible for him to meet his son's every need at all times, and more impossible still to go inside his son's brain and undo his depression. As my friend forgave himself, he connected to a deep sense of unconditional love.

In this exercise, you practice self-forgiveness by first generating compassion for others who have made similar mistakes or been in similar situations.

- ◆ Think of a situation or experience about which you feel guilt, remorse, or contrition.

- ◆ Imagine all the people in the world who are suffering from guilt or remorse for similar reasons.

- ◆ Allow yourself to feel how much these people are suffering as a result of their real or perceived mistakes—even months or years after they've made amends.

- ◆ Allow yourself to feel compassion for them, knowing they did their best. Recognize the ways in which they are being unnecessarily hard on themselves.

- Imagine these people feeling that same sense of compassion toward *you*. Feel their compassion like a warm light spreading through your body. Open yourself up to the possibility that you are worthy of forgiveness, and allow yourself to feel compassion toward yourself.

Repeat this exercise as many times as necessary until you can consistently generate compassion toward yourself.

Chapter 10

THE FREEDOM TO SERVE

Once when I was a child in Mexico, I was walking past a church with my father and my grandmother. My father told me to go inside and pray until I got an answer from an angel. I did as he told me. When I entered the church, I found a statue of an angel, knelt down in front of it, and started praying. After I'd been kneeling there for a while, willing the angel to answer me, I realized that I was praying to *myself*—or rather, my *Self. I* was the only person who could hear my prayer and answer it. I ran back outside and reported this discovery to my father, who smiled. He was always so proud when my brothers and I answered one of his riddles, and this time was no different.

The word *angel* comes from the Greek *angelos,* which means "messenger." My father often says that we are all angels sent to earth to deliver a message, and the message is how we live our lives. Our message manifests as our actions toward others. If we live our lives in a selfish, greedy way, the message we deliver is that greed and selfishness are the proper path. If we live our lives from a place of unconditional love and humility, that becomes our message to the people around us and to the universe at large. We can use our message to serve others and elevate humanity, or we can use it to hurt others and ourselves. It's up to us.

We sometimes have a hard time seeing ourselves as servants of humanity, especially if we perceive that we need special skills to do so. How can we serve if we are not doctors, firefighters, or climate scientists? How can we serve if we are sick, or disabled, or weighed down with responsibilities? How can we serve if we feel lost or imperfect? How can we serve if we've made mistakes in the past, if other people have stopped trusting us, or if we have stopped trusting ourselves?

Many of us have been domesticated to the idea that a life of service is unrealistic or impractical. We are encouraged to devote our lives to making money and acquiring possessions, without pausing to consider whether our work truly benefits our fellow humans, other animals, or Mother Earth herself. The domestication to be materially successful can be so strong that many of us feel that we literally *don't have* the freedom to serve, or that we couldn't tolerate the sacrifices we think we would have to make to be of service. We buy into the dream that material prosperity must come first, and we inadvertently give up our personal freedom in the process.

The good news is that we can *all* be of service, and we don't have to be in a specific profession or give up our existing professions to do so. Being of service is a mindset—an attitude—that you can choose to bring to any encounter, any activity, at any time.

Consider for a moment what your life would be like if you truly felt free to serve. It might not be all that different from what it is now. Or it might look dramatically different. In my case, devoting my life to service only came *after* a long period of searching, wandering, and getting hooked by various dreams. I believe that the nagual within each of us is always looking for a way to serve, and it all starts with opening your heart and mind, and being willing to listen carefully and cooperate when life calls.

Angel Training

I used to believe that I had to maintain a spiritual persona that wasn't true to myself in order to be a good angel—a good messenger. I thought I had to meditate for many hours every day, follow a strict schedule, and abstain from laughing or being silly. I assumed I had to surround myself with "spiritual" books and "spiritual" people, and even with "spiritual" music. Most important, I was convinced that I had to hide my troubled past and the mistakes I had made—my years using drugs and alcohol, my experiences of sexual abuse, my suicide attempt, and my failed relationships. What kind of angel would admit to all of *that*? And besides, how could anyone trust such an angel to deliver a message worth listening to?

Then my father and I collaborated on a book called *The Fifth Agreement*. The idea for this book came to me when my father was in a coma for nine weeks following a heart attack. To carry on his work during this difficult time, I'd started poking through some materials he'd developed called Angel Training. I realized he'd organized this material to unfold in a very slow, sequential, rigorous way. I also noticed that most of his students weren't getting it. So I decided to take these ideas and teach them in a different way—all at once, in one package, going straight to the heart of the matter and discarding the many "levels" my father had outlined.

When my father woke up from his coma, he asked me what I'd been doing with my time. I told him I'd been teaching Angel Training, but not in the way he'd planned. When I showed him what I'd been doing, he laughed out loud and said: "You've just created the Fifth Agreement." And the result of this work was the book by that name.

When the book came out, I knew I'd have to go on a book tour and do a lot of public speaking. I was feeling very nervous about going out in public and my mind began to worry. What would happen if I was exposed as a former drug user, a sexual abuse survivor, a divorced person, or any other negative or shameful thing? This anxiety began to eat away at me, until my partner finally told me it was time to take those skeletons out of my closet. "When you go on book tour," she said, "you should go as yourself."

Her words threw me for a loop. What would happen if I went on tour as the real Jose, not the "spiritual" persona I had created in my mind? What would happen if I spoke openly about my life, instead of hoping people wouldn't find out what I had done or what had happened to me? Could I serve others if I went into the world as this kind of angel? Would my message be lost—or would it be more powerful than ever?

On one of my first stops on the tour, I decided to drop the speech I'd prepared. Instead, I just started talking. I talked about doing drugs on the streets of Tijuana, and about the many painful lessons I'd learned in my relationships with women. I talked about my struggles, my failures, and my moments of grace. As I spoke, I could feel my heart opening and I could tell that the people in the audience could feel it too. Instead of feeling cheated or disappointed by the fact that this supposedly "spiritual" person was admitting to failure, confusion, and mistakes, they seemed inspired.

After the talk was over, several people came up to me to thank me for my authenticity. One man told me that my story had given him hope. "If someone like you can go through all that and still end up *here*," he said, "then I feel as if there's hope for me too."

Now I no longer try to hide what I went through in the past, or what I'm going through in the present. I realize that the fear and shame I felt about my past were actually *preventing* me from being an effective angel and keeping me from serving others in the unique way that I am called. Not only that, but in modeling unconditional love for myself, I make it easier for the people around me to practice unconditional love themselves. As you probably can tell by now, practicing unconditional love *is* my message; it is how I serve.

Most of us have been domesticated to regret our mistakes and display a sense of embarrassment about them, if we ever speak of them at all. We make agreements with ourselves to bury our failures, hide our shortcomings, and live in a state of permanent regret about the things we've said or done that make us cringe. But it's only by being open about our mistakes, failures, and regrets that we can be the most helpful to others. Nothing connects you to the heart of another person like authenticity. Dropping any false persona and letting the real angel that is you shine forth is the quickest way to reach the hearts of others.

Energy as Service

I want to make clear that being of service is not just about physical acts like caring for the sick or picking up trash, although these are wonderful ways in which to serve. Being of service means paying careful attention to the message you are sending through your words, your actions, and the state of your being. In that sense, it means being mindful of your energy and taking responsibility for yourself at a deeper and deeper level, so that even your most insignificant actions take on a quality of service and benevolence.

The shamans of my family recognized a long time ago that energy is contagious. You've likely noticed this already just by watching yourself and others. When you go through life in a state of anxiety, you promote anxiety in those around you. When you undertake an action with the energy of resentment, that resentment will have a harmful effect, no matter how helpful or necessary the action itself may be. But once you recognize that your energy influences others, you naturally become more mindful and more aware of its impact. When a negative state arises, you pause and say: "Okay, I am feeling some resentment. What can I do with this? How can I let it pass in a harmless way?"

You may need to stop what you are doing and go into a room by yourself for a few minutes. Or perhaps you journal about what you're feeling, or call a trusted friend to talk about it, or sit quietly and process the emotions without creating a story of suffering around them. Whatever you do, the important thing is to keep the ball in *your* court instead of making it somebody else's problem. Your task is to deal with that negative energy inside of yourself—although you may ask others for help—so that when it does come out, it has been cleansed of everything harmful.

We've all lived through a global pandemic that made us keenly aware of the principle of contagion. And this principle applies to energy as well as to disease. My family contains both shamans and medical doctors, and they all agree that our energy is like medicine. We all have a fully loaded syringe with which we are constantly injecting our energy into the planet. The question is, what's your syringe going to contain? Are you going to inject the earth with emotional poison? Or are you going to offer it joy, compassion, and love?

When we inject our unconditional love into the Dream of the Planet, it's as if Mother Earth receives the antibodies she needs to combat the negativity, the pain, and the lies that are also being let loose on the planet. When we awaken and live happy and authentic lives, we contribute to the betterment of humanity. Protecting our energy in this way is a form of service.

Working with Energy

Have you ever encountered a total stranger who leaves you feeling wonderful for no apparent reason? There is just something about this person's presence that brightens your day, and you immediately feel elevated, comforted, and fully seen. This is the magic of energy. When you take good care of your own energy, you exist in a state of joy and harmony, and you transmit this state to others. You heal the people around you with your presence.

Think about the last time you felt frustrated, depressed, worried, or angry. What did you do with that feeling? Did you go out into the world with a cloud hanging over your head, sharing that emotional poison with everyone you encountered? Or did you use your awareness to transform that difficult energy into something that was no longer harmful to those around you, let alone yourself? Did you create a story about that feeling? "It's so unfair." "It shouldn't be this way." Or did you commit to experiencing the uncomfortable emotions with love and courage, so that they could burn themselves out in a harmless way?

Whatever energy you cultivate inside yourself has a real effect on those around you, and even ripples out to people you've never met. This is why it's so important to remember the power of your energy. When you maintain awareness and deal with internal states skillfully and compassionately, you avoid sending out messages of anger, hatred, or self-pity into Mother Earth's collective energy pool. Instead, let your message be one of love, wisdom, and gentleness.

When you go into the world with a smile and an open heart, you inspire those qualities in others. This process of inspiration is profound and endless. The more you reflect your love to others, the more their own capacity for love wakes up and reflects itself back to you and the world. Your presence, living in your own personal heaven, can inspire others to light that flame in their heavens.

Exercise: Claiming Your Energy

Every time you take responsibility for your own energy, you take a powerful stand for peace. By refusing to pass your inner disturbances along to others, you become a protector of humanity and transform your own negativity into light—a true act of service.

Here is a simple exercise that can help you do that.

- The next time you notice your energy becoming clouded with anger, resentment, despair, or another "harmful" element, stop whatever you are doing and just notice it.

- Place a hand on your heart and name the feeling. Then say: "I notice you. I see that you are there, and I am going to take good care of you."

- Create space around this difficult energy and imagine it as a tangled ball of yarn, or some other physical shape.

- In your mind, place this imagined object inside a larger container. For example, imagine the tangled ball of yarn sitting at the bottom of a huge bowl, or lying in the middle of a football field.

When you imagine a larger space in which the difficult energy can exist, you tap into your true nature, which is vast, expansive, and strong. You remember that whatever disturbance you are feeling, it is only a tiny blip in the infinite field of loving awareness. Simply holding the disturbance within this larger field is a powerful practice that allows negative energy to transform and go harmlessly on its way.

Exercise: Simple Acts of Service

Sometimes we forget that simple acts of service can enrich our lives and the lives of those around us. These acts break down our self-centeredness and put us in closer connection with our fellow beings. This in turn reduces the mind's addiction to suffering, which cannot survive without some degree of self-centeredness to give it power.

In this exercise, I invite you to conduct simple acts of service throughout your day. Here are some examples, although there are many other possibilities. Feel free to add your own.

- Smile at others.

- Repeat a silent mantra for those you encounter, like: "May this person be happy."

- Give up your seat on the bus or subway.

- Let someone in front of you in line.

- Help a neighbor with a physical task.

- Wash the dishes when you visit someone's home.

- Put away the chairs after a meeting.

- Clean up a mess or make a minor repair, even when it's not your responsibility.

- Give a genuine compliment.

- Listen to someone's story with empathy, even if you don't agree with everything he or she is saying.

◆ Do an exquisite job on any task, no matter how trivial or menial.

When you perform simple acts of service, you express your love for the earth, for your fellow human beings, and for life itself.

If you want to take this exercise a step further, you can make a gentle wish every time you perform an act of service. For example, if you give up your seat on the bus or subway, make a wish like: "May this person rest deeply and gain strength for the day ahead." If you help your neighbor unload some heavy boxes, make a wish like: "May my neighbor always have the support she needs." When you wish good things for others, you add the energy of love to your act of service, and remind yourself of the fundamental unity of life.

Conclusion

THE GIFT OF FREEDOM

When you've been walking the path of personal freedom for some time, there comes a point when you begin to see everybody and everything as a part of yourself. You see yourself in the beggar, the flight attendant, and the grocery checkout clerk. You see yourself in your friends and family, as well as in the people you may have formerly considered your enemies. The whole world starts to feel like a part of your own body, and you are filled with the desire to care for it tenderly. Although others may have different perspectives, or use different words, or have different beliefs, or speak different languages, you know that they are all just shapeshifting from light into light— like the flickering flame of a candle. You know that the same precious gift that was given to you when you were born was also given to everyone around you. We are all doing our best to care for our piece of the nagual.

Once you've had the experience of seeing yourself and others as one ever-changing body of light, many of the old difficulties of life fall away. It becomes much harder to judge others, or become angry with them, or especially to hate them, because you've stopped judging and hating yourself. You can see the flicker of divinity in every person, even when they are doing something you don't like. You get more and more skilled at seeing beyond the layers of defenses that people put over their hearts, and the masks they pull over their faces.

When you are aware of the oneness of us all, it becomes much less likely that you will become upset when things don't go as you intend. You realize that whatever happens, you can fold it into the artwork of your life. Nothing can ruin your masterpiece, because you have the power to integrate any experience into your art. Even if someone knocks over the ink or splatters the paint, it doesn't matter. It's still perfect. When you are a master artist, you possess the power of creation inside you and know that no matter how many obstacles arise, you will never run out of beauty. No matter where you go, you carry this power with you, so you never have to fear the inevitable surprises of life.

As your heart opens wider and wider, it can hold more and more. You can hold your own mistakes with love and compassion. You don't need to deny them or bury them. You can admit to your own wrongdoings and weaknesses, because you have no fear of being judged by yourself or anyone else. You can hold other people's pain and sorrow with greater compassion, knowing these things are only temporary reflections in the mirror. You stop judging others, having realized that they are only dreaming. You give unconditional love to yourself and others, regardless of the mistakes they have made, while holding the boundaries you need to keep yourself safe.

The Dream of the Shaman

Shamans know that we are all dreaming all the time, and realize that most people don't know it. But here is the paradox. Even as shamans know at the deepest level that this is a dream, we simultaneously recognize the suffering that exists in the phenomenal world.

We acknowledge that there is real oppression in the world—real violence, real inequality, real slavery. These struggles are not imaginary, and they require the collective effort of many to overcome them. The quest for personal freedom is not an alternative to these struggles, but rather the most important path you can take to help end them. You can be a more effective champion of justice if you have overcome your own negativity, your own addiction to suffering, and your own lies and delusions. You can make greater contributions to the Dream of the Planet if you've eliminated the seeds of violence within yourself, and given up the vain striving to glorify a self that at the deepest level doesn't really exist.

As you walk this path, you know to respect the dreams of others without trying to change them, and you use your own agreements to live a good life. What others take so seriously, shamans see as simply playful ideas in a dream—race, gender, nation-states, and the many other agreements that organize human societies. They are like visitors from another planet, learning human customs without believing in them completely or being bound by them.

I often say that Jose is the love of my life, and that my number one job in this lifetime is to take care of him and make him happy. At the same time, I know that Jose doesn't really exist. He's a figure of speech, a story, a reflection in the mirror. Knowing that Jose doesn't really exist, it doesn't matter if I am rich or poor, famous or unknown, doing this job or that one. I am available to serve life, because I *am* life. Whatever I do, wherever I go, I'm serving life. So there is no worry, nothing to be afraid of, and certainly no regrets.

Like a Buddhist bodhisattva—an awakened one who stays here on earth to serve others—a nagual uses their freedom for the greater good. This is not a hard duty to assume, because once you become a nagual, you naturally want to help others.

As you walk the path to your own personal freedom, how will you serve life? Will you use your freedom to create beautiful artwork? To fight for justice? To preserve nature for future generations? Will you serve life with your voice? Your heart? Your hands? The power of your mind? If you don't know yet, I'm sure you will find out. You have the light within you, and the path is already unfolding to lead you there. You are walking with five hundred ancestors behind you.

ABOUT THE AUTHOR

don Jose Ruiz is a *Nagual* (Toltec shaman) in the Eagle Knights lineage and the son of don Miguel Ruiz, author of *The Four Agreements*. Jose is the author of *The Medicine Bag*, *The Wisdom of the Shamans*, and *Shamanic Power Animals*. He is also the co-author of *The Fifth Agreement*.

San Antonio, TX

www.hierophantpublishing.com